Pathways of Prayer

Pathways of Prayer

A Lent Course

Edited by

GRAHAM DOW

with contributions from

Cardinal Basil Hume
Grace Sheppard
Donald English
Gerard W. Hughes
Angela Tilby

Illustrations by Sarah John

DARTON · LONGMAN + TODD

First published in 1996 by
Darton, Longman and Todd Ltd
1 Spencer Court
140–142 Wandsworth High Street
London SW18 4JJ

Reprinted 1997 (4th printing)

ISBN 0–232–52183–2

A catalogue record for this book is available
from the British Library

Unless otherwise stated, The Scripture quotations in this
publication are taken from The Jerusalem Bible published
and copyright 1966, 1967 and 1968 by Darton, Longman and Todd Ltd
and Doubleday and Co. Inc.

Design by Sandie Boccacci
Phototypeset in 10/11½pt Times by Intype London Ltd
Printed and bound in Great Britain by
BPC Wheatons Ltd, Exeter

My Special Thanks to:

Morag Reeve, my editor at Darton, Longman and Todd,
for her encouragement to write this book.

Those who produced the Willesden Area Study Course
and were willing for me to adapt it for publication.
  Raymond Avent
  Molly Dow
  Robert Harrison (also much help with this book)
  Liz Shedden

My staff
  Nikki Nelson
  Christine White

The members of my Prayer Circle, who constantly
support all my ministry in prayer.

This book is dedicated to the clergy and people of the
Anglican congregations in the Willesden area of the
London Diocese, who received the Year for Prayer so
enthusiastically.

Contents

Introduction

Our generation is marked by a growing thirst to discover the art of prayer. What is causing this is hard to discern clearly, but there is a growing sense of dissatisfaction with a life based largely on materialism, on acquiring more and more possessions, and in larger and better furnished homes. Overwork is a dehumanising feature of our day. Market forces with acute competition and the need to deliver measurable results are creating more stress in family life. On the other hand there are many people who face the serious financial anxiety that comes with unemployment. Churches are finding that people have less time and energy than before to attend midweek meetings, and leaders for youth organisations are increasingly hard to find. Also, in spite of all our technology the process of living takes up a great deal of our time.

For these reasons there is an instinctive yearning for peace, for things eternal, things that will still be there when everything else is shaken. Our human delusions of grandeur are exposed; we recognise that we simply cannot be self-sufficient in God's world. We must pray.

There is also a growing sense of moral and spiritual anxiety. There is no longer an agreed framework of spiritual beliefs about God. Western society, tragically, is in the process of setting aside its long held beliefs about Jesus Christ as Son of God, the one who was sent from heaven as teacher and pattern of human life and the one through whom wrongdoing is cancelled and forgiven. Sin, now, is hardly mentioned at all.

Everyone is to have their own individual religious

beliefs, if they have any at all. Religion is thought to be a personal matter, and the truth, or otherwise, of different beliefs is not faced. Moral values, correspondingly, have also become more of a personal matter, with the loss of clear moorings held by everyone. In general we have lost the sense of being accountable for our lives, unless it is just simply being accountable to ourselves. We are adrift at sea, without clear beliefs, morals or direction and young people in particular feel it most of all.

In the face of these uncertainties the Spirit of God is making many people restless. God is putting into our hearts and minds a desire for spiritual realities. Courses on prayer are well attended. If moral and spiritual darkness is descending, the answer, of course, lies not with more programmes and activity but with light. Light is with God; for God is light. It will always be the people who pray who are the people of light. It is the people who pray who guard the true realities in a nation when many believe that they can manage without them. Whatever the future holds, it is this instinct to learn to pray, to find space for quiet and for retreats, which is well founded. The Spirit of God is calling us to return to prayer.

This course on personal prayer aims to help people grow in their experience of prayer. It is not about praying as a group, valuable though that is. It seeks to offer a variety of pathways for developing a personal relationship with God. Since we are all very different from one another, what is the most helpful pathway for one person is not the most helpful way for another. God is the creator of all that we are. He invites us to relate to him with our whole being, and from time to time to explore new ways of praying. This will keep a sense of adventure and freshness. Like all other real relationships, the relationship with God only prospers as it grows.

Taking Part in this Course

The Course

The original group study course around which this book is based was a course used in the Willesden area of the Anglican Diocese of London in Lent 1995, entitled *Pathways of Prayer*. It has been rewritten so that for each of its five themes, an interview has been conducted with a well-known Christian leader or author, in which they shared unhurriedly some of their experience of prayer. Many of these insights have then been used in the five main chapters of the book to illustrate important aspects of the journey of prayer. A cassette is also available offering short recorded interviews with the same five Christian people. The study outlines included in this book make provision for the playing of the short recorded interview during each group session.

The aim of the course is to help people to grow in their personal prayer life. It explores ways of developing a deeper two-way relationship with God, and introduces different ways of praying.

Taking Part

It is hoped that the course will enable all who take part to become more open and 'real' in their dealings with God. It seeks to enable them to try out new ways of praying, to develop a greater desire for God himself, and to grow in confidence in their relationship with him.

While the course can be done on one's own, it is written for use in groups. Because we differ a great deal as people, so we do in our experience of God. We can enrich others and be enriched by them as we dare to talk about our experiences of him. We find that we are not as alone in our experience as perhaps we thought, and we get good ideas for our own journey from those who have already followed similar paths.

It is also important to set aside time on a daily basis to follow through some of the exercises offered. This will help to build good patterns of daily prayer which will continue to provide a firm basis for communion with God long after the group has ceased.

Group sessions are intended to last about an hour and three quarters. Between six and ten people is about the best size for a group discussing personal things like prayer.

During the Week Before the Group

1. Read the chapter for the coming session. The discussion will be better if everyone present has read the chapter beforehand.
2. From week 2 onwards, do some of the prayer exercises at the end of the previous session. About ten to fifteen minutes a day for these is ideal. Through exploring a variety of methods you will discover what will be helpful to you in the future.

At the Group

1. You will not be asked to bare your soul! Rather, you will be invited to share your experience just as you wish to.
2. Do not judge the experiences of other people. Concentrate rather on listening and affirming what they have shared. To react in a judgemental way will

make people close up very quickly. Of course our experience of God is very limited and our understanding will not always be complete. The contributors to this book show some differences of opinion. The most important thing is that we pray, letting God teach us as we go on the journey.

3. The study outline can be adapted in order to suit the needs of the group. A guide for group leaders is included as Appendix 1.

If You are Doing the Course on Your Own

1. Try and set aside an uninterrupted hour during the week, as well as time day by day for the prayer exercises. If an hour is impossible take each session in two or three parts.

2. Find someone to talk about the course with, either a Christian friend, or your pastor. Speak openly with them about what you are finding helpful and what you are finding hard. Some Christians ask an experienced person to be their spiritual director or soul friend to meet with three or four times a year and to share their spiritual journey with them. After completing the course you might wish to look for such a person.

The Meaning of the Symbols

 prayer or reflection on your own, in silence

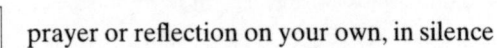 sharing and discussion in pairs (or threes)

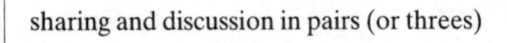 discussion in the full group, led by the group leader

Session 1

Getting Started
with Cardinal Basil Hume

Basil Hume is the Cardinal Archbishop of Westminster and head of the Roman Catholic Church in England and Wales. After his school years at Ampleforth College, at the age of eighteen he joined the Benedictine Community there as a novice. Much of his life has been spent teaching in the college, but later he became the Abbot of the Community. He moved to Westminster as Archbishop in 1976.

I met the Cardinal at his London home and asked him how he learnt to pray.

> My mother, being French and very Roman Catholic, we were brought up to say morning and night prayers. Then, going to a Catholic school, prayer was part of the routine of school life. In those days, you went to Mass, (or the Eucharist), every morning. It was compulsory. And then there were morning and night prayers, and prayers before the beginning of study; and the whole sort of atmosphere of being in a monastic school clearly was prayer-oriented.
>
> I think the interesting question is, when does one move from saying prayers to actually praying. I wouldn't want to pretend that saying prayers is not praying – it is. But there comes a time, I think, when your mind and heart become more involved in what you are doing. That comes with maturity. Probably all of us have to start with the routine of using words, whether it is the Lord's Prayer, or prayers out of a book. That's how I started.

People start to pray for a great variety of reasons. Some are taught to pray by their parents, or, perhaps, by an aunt or a godparent. Some learn at school. Some are bowled over by an experience in church and start to respond. Some pray very little until they are faced with a crisis and need help beyond themselves. Some experience wonder at a sunrise or sunset, or in seeing the beauty of nature, or the majesty of the stars, and they know that there is someone or something very great. Whatever the way in, we learn to see that it began, not with our own initiative, but with God who first moved us to pray. He prompted us, either revealing himself in some way, or putting in us the desire to pray. And we responded; we prayed.

The Cardinal defined prayer like this: it is *trying to raise my heart and mind to God*. Without God first reaching out to us this would be quite impossible. There is no way that human beings, left to themselves, can make contact with God. However, God is longing for us to know him. He opens a way and his Spirit is ready to assist us. We have to respond to the nudges and step into it.

Prayer is 'coming home', (to use Richard Foster's phrase). God invites us to return to where we belong, to come home, to be with him, home to that for which we were created. We have forgotten him. Yet when we return, he welcomes us home to serenity and peace and joy, to friendship, to the intimacy and affirmation that we all need. Prayer is the route home. The 'pathways of prayer', which are offered in these studies for Lent are, therefore, pathways to home.

A Variety of Pathways

Speaking

There is plenty of variety in these pathways and we must learn to choose those that suit our make-up. *Speaking*, for many people, is an obvious place to start in raising mind and heart to God. A great many early experiences of prayer are spoken. Sadly, however, many people think of prayer only in terms of speaking and many other rich pathways to home are ignored.

Thinking

For Cardinal Hume it was through reflection, through just *thinking* about important life experiences, that he began his discovery of the importance of prayer. Then prayer began to take on a deeper meaning than simply saying prayers. This happened by being faced with issues, first of death, and then of happiness, of beauty and of love.

> The first one was experience of death, experience of seeing a coffin, and that was a very powerful thing. That was when I was very, very young, and I remember asking, 'What is that, and why do people have to die?' And I think that the impression has never quite left me, the idea that life is very short.

The next significant point of awareness came in a practice exam, when an essay had to be written in three hours on 'happiness'.

> It was a very good exercise because we had to think out, 'What do you think about happiness? What is happiness?' I found that quite effective because it made me realise that a lot of people weren't happy, and that it was always a transient thing. It was very difficult to hang on to it once you had it; disappointment was always what it seemed to be. I think that was quite an experience, at the age of just seventeen.

The experience of God as present in beauty came to the Cardinal through the reading of poetry like Wordsworth's work about Tintern Abbey, and other works of Wordsworth and Coleridge. God shows himself through artistry; human beings are in his image and their artistry reflects his. The experience of love came with the normal giddy experiences of youth and their connection with feelings of happiness. The important point, however, is that reflecting on all these experiences

5

served to raise mind and heart to God. They raised questions about God. They pointed to his living reality. They made the soul say 'yes' to God. The experience, plus the reflection, turned out to be a pathway of prayer.

Further paths emerged as the Cardinal went on to speak of looking, listening, feeling and writing as ways of praying.

Looking

I think you can pray with your eyes and with your ears, and you pray with the way you feel, but always with God as a reference. So I think just looking at a crucifix is a powerful prayer. My experience of hospital is very limited, but one thing I have learnt is that it is jolly difficult to pray there. And so, when people are terminally ill, or very ill, then I say the only prayer you can make is the kissing of the crucifix. It's a marvellous prayer! You don't need to do anything else.

Listening

I think if you go into a church and you've got a marvellous choir and you just listen to that choir, I think it carries your mind and heart up to God. It just does it. It just happens. You are enjoying the music. It somehow or other concentrates the mind and heart.

All the human senses can be involved in our praying and all the aspects of human experience. We are complex, but whole people. Important though the mind is, it is not the whole of us, as experiences such as loving and grieving make clear. God relates to the whole of us, and many pathways of prayer are possible. Different approaches will suit us at different times. Sometimes we need few words and more silence. Sometimes, we just need to 'be' with God, perhaps sensing that we are in his arms, or that he is beside us. We need not be afraid of such mental imagery, even if there is the possibility of creating God just as we want him to be rather than as he is. We are raising mind *and heart* to God.

Nor should it surprise us that there are so many pathways. God is known in all that he has made. It is the different human senses that put us in touch with the richness of God's universe.

Feeling

A lot of people, who are agonising for one reason or another, they often cannot use words. Words don't come. So I think that you have to be, as it were, in the presence of God, feeling wretched. Some may say to them to go and chat to God about it – often they don't know how to chat. They don't want words; words don't work; they are too limited. So I just say, all you need is just to be, in the presence of God.

For prayer which is feeling a visual focus can be very helpful. Looking and feeling go together well. A picture or icon of Christ may be evocative, or simply a lit candle. We may try sitting quietly in an upright chair giving space for the feelings. Tears may come which are always healing.

Writing

Writing is a mode of praying which I find extremely helpful, especially when one is over wrought, or there is too much on your mind, or you've got a worry in your head when there are too many distractions. I find I sit down and write my prayer. I find that a terrific thing! I tear it up pretty quickly afterwards. But just to write out what's going through the mind, like a letter to God, and then you know afterwards that you have prayed about that. I don't know what to do about this, so I write it out.

I learnt this from St Thérèse of Lisieux, the Carmelite. On the door of her cell she had scratched, '*Dieu est mon unique amour*' [God is my only love]. And she went through a dark night of the soul towards the end of her life. It's very interesting because when she was beatified [made blessed], the nuns covered it up because you couldn't have saints indulging in graffiti, even high-powered graffiti! Now the covering has been removed. I have been in her cell and I've actually seen it.

So God takes the initiative and he moves us to pray. We can respond in a great many ways, as we wish, but it is important to keep before us the sense that it is for God that we are doing it. We need a sense of freedom about how we pray. God has called us children, and children have a natural curiosity and playfulness about them. They are inventive. So we can be with God. We do not have to pray in a particular way. We can light a candle, sing a song or a hymn, or put on a CD that moves us inwardly. We may shout for joy or be very quiet. We should be real and hide nothing. If we are angry, we can vent that anger at God. Relationships can be wonderfully varied and God's home is big enough for all of us in great diversity. It is one of the great sadnesses of Christian history that so many believers have become trapped in stereotyped and unfulfilling forms of prayer, when all that is needed is a little imagination and freedom.

But prayer can be hard and boring too, and there are lots of times when we don't really want to pray. Cardinal Hume shared his experience of this.

There are moments when it is tedious, and the trouble is that people who go into a tedious moment, or find there's nothing happening, or no return of prayer, that's when they give it up. That's when we have to stick at it! You stick at it because you are not doing it to enjoy yourself, you are doing it for an entirely different motive – to please God.

We pray because God wants us to pray; he wants us to relate to him. And we pray because this is how to pursue the relationship with him into which he has invited us. Moreover, it is for our own good that we live life in harmony and relationship with the world's creator. Given all the positive reasons it is a wonder that we do not pray more! But then, it takes a while for the fruit of prayer to be apparent.

Advice to Someone Starting to Pray

I asked the Cardinal what advice he would give to someone who was just beginning to learn to pray.

I tell them first of all to decide, 'Am I going to do this every day? Am I going to spend whatever number of minutes are available?' It may be 2, 3, 4 minutes, or even less. But then I say, 'Take a prayer you know, such as the "Our Father", and just say it slowly. Just think about each of the phrases: "Our Father – ", just think about that. And you may want to go no further, you may want to rest on that. And then you go on to the next phrase.'

Or you take another prayer that you like and enjoy: one that you know, and then you take it bit by bit.

And I think that posture is quite important. If you are young and can kneel easily, it is quite a good thing to kneel.

But you make up your mind to do that regularly. I

9

always say, 'There's no correct way to pray, but the way that is correct for you is the right way.'

Many people find it helpful in developing the daily routine to pray in the same place and to make that place just a little bit special. We may try a particular chair to sit in or a bed to kneel at. Lighting a candle, or placing a cross on the wall or table, helps to remind us that this is a special time; it is time for drawing close to the great and holy one, our God and Father, and to Jesus Christ, his Son.

We may choose different body positions for prayer. These also say something to God. Kneeling expresses our awareness of someone far greater, our penitence, and our need for mercy and forgiveness. Standing expresses alertness and a readiness to go as God's representative to wherever he may send us. To lie prostrate is to recognise that we depend on God totally and can only be anything as he lifts us up. There are times when it is meaningful to sit, or to walk.

Every relationship is different. There are no fixed rules about when and where to relate to God. A prayer relationship with God which is healthy will have in it moments of praise and worship, moments of confession of the wrong we have done, moments of thanksgiving, moments of asking for what we need, and for the needs of the world, and moments of quiet and listening. We read the Scriptures to open ourselves to the word God has already spoken, the word through which he continues to speak, pouring light into the stresses and confusion of our busy lives. When you are starting out to pray, try and find time also for a short meditation from the Bible. Ask your priest or minister for guidance as to how and where to start.

The Journey to Home

We have described prayer as a journey to home. The Cardinal took this up saying that prayer is often sitting by the roadside, just pausing before you take up the journey again. One of his favourite passages for leading into prayer is the story of Bartimaeus (Mark 10:46–52):

> I often start with the story of Bartimaeus because I think that is marvellous. A chap who was born blind on the road to Jericho and he gets his sight restored. Then he follows the Lord. I find that quite a good starting-point for prayer because it's wanting the Lord to touch your eyes so that you can see more clearly, so that you may follow more securely.

The story is an excellent model of the way in which to approach both Scripture reading and prayer. Jesus, the Son of God, shows how great the heart of God is to help us. 'What do you want me to do for you?' he said to the blind man when he cried out. 'Master, let me see again', the man replied. Every time we open the Scriptures or pray, the same words can help us. Jesus is here to help us, and we say, 'Master, let me see.'

We are called to be disciples, those who follow Christ. Prayer is not only the time by the roadside, the pauses, the refreshment points in the journey, it is also the energy supply of the journey itself, the movement to home, into God himself.

What can we hope for as we come to pray? Can we legitimately expect anything? The Archbishop continued.

> I think one can legitimately hope and expect that, if you are seriously beginning to pray, in some manner God will come to meet you. It may just be some sense of well-being, a sense of satisfaction. We were always taught as novices that you seek the God of consolation, not the consolations of God. But that, if

you seek God, then consolations will come. And we were also taught that quite often there was more consolation at the beginning of your praying life than later on. Sometimes it got rougher later on; but that was God, as it were, beckoning you through, so that you became completely orientated towards God and not towards yourself.

What is the fruit of regular prayer? Thousands of fellow travellers throughout the centuries testify to its rich benefits. Many experience a growing understanding of life and its meaning, along with clarity in the decisions they need to take. Different areas of life begin to take on a new quality, a purpose, a joy, a beauty that had not been sensed before. Even through the times of severe difficulty which most Christians experience at one time or another, there is often a growing awareness that God has a purpose in mind for us through the pain, and that keeping going at the routine of prayer, however short the time, is helpful. These large numbers of Christians on the journey would have given up prayer long ago, if it gave no sense of fulfilment. On the other hand there are many who, as the years go by, find that they want more and more of it. This bears out the wisdom of the book of Proverbs:

> in every course you take, have him in mind:
> he will see that your paths are smooth.
>
> (Proverbs 3:6)

Hard Times in Prayer

The Cardinal offered his own insights about the times of darkness on the journey of prayer, the times when God seems to be absent.

It can take different forms. It can take the form of a trial of faith. I mean, is it all true? I don't think I've

12

had that so much, but I have had the experience, which I think some people go through, of asking 'Am I really acceptable to God? Am I really so full of faults, so full of weaknesses, and all the rest of it?' So a lot of the psychological problems which most of us have in some form or another, I think constitute that dark night where the reality of God seems very distant. It is part of prayer for a lot of people. Those who have a serious life of prayer will meet periods of darkness, I think, because if the high point of Christian life is charity, the love of God and neighbour, then charity increases as faith is purified. Faith has to be purified so that in the end there is nothing that really matters in your life except God. You've got to get to the point where you have to trust God absolutely, which I've never achieved.

In the times when God does not seem to be there, then, first, we need to remember that he is there, whatever our feelings may be. He has promised not to leave us. We must not take our feelings as a reliable guide to whether or not he is present. Our feelings are simply our feelings. The presence of God is determined by who he is and what he has promised. 'Seek the God of consolations', the novices were taught, 'not the consolations of God.'

The bottom line is that we pray for God, not for ourselves. We pray because it pleases God that we pray; it is his will. However, the universal Christian testimony is that it brings deep fulfilment. It brings us to home, to God, himself, and to the blessings of his friendship. In Augustine's well-known prayer, 'You made us for yourself, and our hearts are restless until they rest in you.' The hard times are still worth it; we learn to keep going, and God is pleased.

Whatever the difficult times may bring, according to

the Cardinal those setting out on the journey of prayer can do so with firm expectancy.

> I think it is legitimate for a person to expect some gift from God which you can experience as well-being: joy to be there, satisfaction that I have done something which I know is worthwhile, perhaps even a lightness of heart, that a little anxiety which I have doesn't really matter compared to what God has given. I think it's modest, but it's important.

GROUP STUDY

Make sure that everyone in the group knows everyone else's name. If the group has been formed especially for this course, tell one another, briefly, why you are part of the group. Share around the group your expectations (hopes and fears) of the course.

Where have we come from?

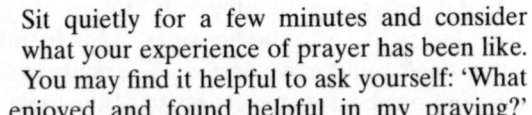 To get to where we are today, each of us has already made a unique, personal journey with God. We started in different places and we began to pray for a variety of reasons; because our parents taught us to pray, or because we needed God's help. In pairs, explain to one another how and why you began to pray.

In the group, briefly make a list of all your answers.

Sit quietly for a few minutes and consider what your experience of prayer has been like. You may find it helpful to ask yourself: 'What have I enjoyed and found helpful in my praying?' 'What have I found difficult?' 'Does any particular experience of prayer stand out as a highlight?'

Where are we now?

 In the group, consider the question, 'Why do I pray now?' You will find that in different situations and in different times, you pray for various reasons. You may find that sometimes your motivation to pray is selfless and at other times it is selfish. Make a list of the group's answers.

You will probably find that several of your answers, perhaps all of them, are to do with developing your relationship with God in various ways. This is not surprising, since prayer is about our relationship with God.

 Look up **Romans 8:15–16 and 26–7**. What do these verses tell us about God's part in our desire to pray?

If you are using the cassette, listen now to the interview with Cardinal Hume. This will refresh your memory about points made in this chapter.

 In pairs, discuss in what ways the Cardinal's experience of learning to pray compared to your own. What was similar and what was different?

 In the group, consider the different ways of praying described in this chapter and on the tape. Which have you found most helpful?

The next section looks at the features that make up our relationship with God in prayer. You may choose to move directly to 'Where do we want to be?' on p. 17.

❦

Something to read

Christian prayer is communication with God through Jesus Christ, and includes many ways of expressing our relationship with him.

God wants to relate to us. That is why he sent Jesus to be born as one of us, to live a perfect human life, to be put to death for our sake and to rise up out of death. God offers us the possibility of knowing him, and, when we have responded to his offer with belief and trust, the relationship has begun.

This relationship with God is so fundamental to human well-being that the Bible says that knowing God is eternal life (John 17:3), which is what God wants for everyone.

Although God does not promise his friends an easy passage through this life, the Christian experience is that he is a better and a closer friend than any other and that he is well worth getting to know. It is through prayer that our relationships with God are healed, deepened and enriched.

⌒⌒

Like any human relationship, our relationship with God has various aspects and ingredients. Here is a list of some of the things that make up a good relationship
    enjoying each other's company
    talking about yourself
    sharing each other's interests
    listening to one another
    sharing each other's problems
    asking for help for someone
    being available to help
    doing things together
    thinking things through together
    conflict
    saying we are sorry
    forgiving the other
    letting off steam
    thinking about the past
    planning for the future
    commitment to each other

Look at this list and discuss how many of these things are part of your prayers. You may wish to add some more. Discuss which are the best bits, which are the most difficult and which tend to be the most neglected.

Talk about how you listen to God, enjoy his company and how you let off steam to him.

A good relationship is one in which we are as honest and open as possible. It is likely to have some ups and downs, but these can be worked through in a constructive way. In pairs, discuss why we can sometimes be afraid to be ourselves, and put on 'masks', even with our friends. How far does this also happen in our relationship with God?

Where do we want to be?

In the light of the things that you have been discussing, think (or dream!) about what you want your relationship with God to become.

Tell God, silently, how you are feeling now and what you long for in your relationship with him. Thank him for giving you a desire to pray. Ask him to help you. Wait in silence, trying to sense his response.

Consider how much time you realistically think you will be able to set aside for prayer during the next few weeks of this course. If possible, a regular time each day is best. Think what time would be most suitable for you. You may find that it helps to tell another member of the group – it will help you to keep to your commitment.

End the meeting by saying these prayers together:

Thanks be to you, O Lord Jesus Christ,
for all the benefits which you have given us,
for all the pains and insults which you have borne
   for us.

O most merciful Redeemer, Friend and Brother,
may we know you more clearly,
love you more dearly, and follow you more nearly,
day by day. Amen.

May the grace of our Lord, Jesus Christ,
the love of God,
and the fellowship of the Holy Spirit
be with us all, evermore. Amen.

DURING THE WEEK

In your prayer time each day, try to include:

- some time talking to God about the things that have
  occupied your thoughts and feelings during the past
  twenty-four hours.
- some time listening to what God may have to say to
  you. Do this by spending some time in silence and
  by reading the Bible.

    Either continue with any Bible reading notes or
    lectionary that you are already using.

    Or choose one of the following passages.
    Isaiah 41:8–10
    Isaiah 49:15–16
    John 14:15–24
    John 15:1–11
    John 15:12–17
- Read chapter 2 of this book, 'Praying through
  Words'.

Session 2

Praying through Words

with Grace Sheppard

Our Father
who art in
Heaven
Hallowed
be thy
name

In the previous chapter, Cardinal Hume gave us a definition of prayer as *trying to raise my heart and mind to God*. As we seek to do this all our senses can be involved. Prayer happens through touching, listening and feeling, just as much as through words. It happens in silence when no words are in mind; we are just there, with God.

All this is to emphasise that our use of words is to be in a perfectly natural context, as we explore the relationship with God. We are seeking to communicate with him in a variety of ways.

Grace Sheppard is an author and broadcaster. She is married to David Sheppard, the Bishop of Liverpool. Before moving to Liverpool, twenty-one years ago, they lived in London: first in Islington, then to Canning Town and the Mayflower Family Centre where David was to be the Warden. They were the first married couple to set up home in the centre. They then moved across the river to Peckham with their daughter Jenny, where David took up his post as Bishop of Woolwich. Grace describes her battle with cancer and agoraphobia during those years and her journey to wholeness and freedom, in her first book, *An Aspect of Fear*.

I met with Grace in her home in Woolton Park near Liverpool, on a sunny morning in June 1996. For her it is clear that her use of words in prayer has to be understood as part of a pattern that has many other facets to it – silence, looking, touch, imagination. Particularly interesting is the way in which, throughout the day, the different approaches play their part.

She explained her regular patterns of prayer.

I have some regular patterns and many irregular patterns. My bedroom window faces the rising of the sun. I always look at the sun and experience it at that moment as a kind of prayer, although without words. So I start the day waiting for the sun to rise.

If I cannot see it I know it is still there, and it's a kind of blessing to me – God rising to greet me, so to speak; and I try to greet him in that way. Those are wordless moments; occasionally words will come out if it's a particularly lovely day.

Ideally, I spend the next hour with a cup of tea and with silence, a book or two, with the Bible, and often I write.

At 8.30 a.m. Grace meets with David, with his chaplain, and with the gardener, for the morning office. This is an Anglican liturgy; the four participants begin by lighting a candle, and with a short period of silence. The readings are discussed and as well as prayers from the service book there is a place for offering prayers in their own words. So, already, heart and mind have been raised to God through stillness and silence as well as through words, mostly the given words of the liturgy. Grace describes this time of the morning office as their bedrock.

Conversational Prayer

As the day moves on, her praying takes up a conversational style.

My praying changes into much more of a conversation with a friend. I feel very thankful for the way I was brought up. My mother enjoyed praying with us and taught us to regard Jesus as a friend. It was only later on that I decided that I wanted to pray to him as Father. It became much more natural to me, and now I relate to him as Friend and Father, and Mother and Grandmother. All sorts of people are caught up in this being called God, to me.

For instance, we can hear the wren in the garden as we speak. I relate, then, to God as my Creator and I thank him for these beautiful sounds. I thank him for my hearing, I thank him for my sight because I can see the wren from my kitchen window. We live in a beautiful place; we've been given many wonderful blessings; and out of that arises a constant 'thank you'. I have plenty of times, also, when I complain. But, the Creator God is there; the Father God is there, the one who protects me; the Mother God is there, the one who enfolds me, the Brother and Sister God, the one who walks alongside me.

The striking thing about this pattern of prayer is its naturalness. As with most human relationships, it is natural in the prayer relationship for words to be very central. Yet if we think of prayer as simply saying prayers, we lose the sense of being real with God. The words take their place in the interplay which involves all our God-given senses in raising heart and mind to him. God, however, is more than a human being. He is very great and to be held in awe. There are times when we want to say very little. We do well to note the advice of the preacher, in the book of Ecclesiastes,

> Be in no hurry to speak; do not hastily declare yourself before God; for God is in heaven, you on earth. Be sparing, then, of speech. (Ecclesiastes 5:1)

Somehow, there is a balance to be struck between the naturalness of speaking words towards a God who accepts us completely, and the silence appropriate to being in the presence of majesty.

Grace continued:

> I know I often say, 'Oh God!', which to some people sounds like swearing, but actually, for me, it's a prayer. I am actually directing it to God. And I refuse to give that up just because it sounds like a swear word, because to me it's really important. I suppose I get something out of my system to him. It's part of the relationship.

Prayer means that you are never alone. I always have a 'good companion'. I think that is important nowadays. So many of us are needing to know that we are not alone and yet we are becoming more and more individualistic. More people than ever are buying homes to live by themselves.

The words that we use in prayer, then, are those that flow naturally towards our 'good companion'. Many find it particularly helpful to focus that friendship in addressing prayer to Jesus. We think of him as the one who is with us all day and every day. He is the companion on the journey, and he is also the 'home' to which we journey.

Grace illustrated the kind of things she might say to Jesus during the day.

Something like, 'Lord, my shoulder is hurting.' I put my shoulder out a few years ago. I just tell him that it's hurting; and then I fancy that he says, 'Well, what do you want to do about that?' And I say, 'I would like you to come into my shoulder and be there with me in that pain.' It actually causes me to relax, extraordinarily, and it becomes a bit of a healing moment for me. I have noticed that if I am sitting badly in a chair and I begin to ache in various places, if I tell God that I am feeling a bit tired, he will be there for me, and I will be able to adjust the way I sit. This kind of prayer is very practical.

Before I am going to speak at a meeting, I get incredibly nervous beforehand. I tell him exactly how I am feeling and then I start to pray for the people I am going to speak to and somehow he lifts me out of myself; I begin to look forward to seeing God in other people. My apprehension turns into excitement. I then want to get out there.

At times of crisis, all that we have learnt about this daily relationship is there for us to draw on. Grace spoke about one particular occasion, at the time of her breakdown in 1957.

I collapsed in an underground station and landed up in the medical centre in Islington. There were people around me whom I knew, but I could not speak to them properly, and I found myself just saying, 'Jesus, Jesus, Jesus'. That's what came out of me and it anchored me at that very frightening time. I was all over the place; I was terrified; I didn't know what was happening. I thought I was dying. Totally uncoordinated, I felt. And I recalled, I think it was in Kenya, during the years of the Mau Mau, when I must have read that one of the missionaries found herself doing just this. I remember lying flat on this sort of hard table in the medical centre recalling the missionary at her frightening moment and when she just said, 'Jesus, Jesus', and somehow, I was given those words, simple as they are. It was a terrifying moment, but a good moment, and I am thankful for whatever it was that enabled me to speak them.

Thanksgiving

What are the things that we really want to say to God? We need a focus for our words. It may be a cry for help. It may be thanksgiving. It may be to confess what we have done wrong. It may be to pray for others. It may be words of praise or adoration. For Grace, the experience of her healing has led her to be very easily moved to thanksgiving. Often, the words follow after the awareness of God's goodness has come through one of the other senses.

If you walk out into my garden now, I can take you

to a lavender bush and we can smell it. That reminds me of God's love. It makes me feel that there is something good out there, that has been put there for me and for us. So if you can't find words, then try one of the other senses and let God speak through those. Then you will find this 'thank you' coming up. Once the 'thank you' words start to pour out, we are into praise, we are into worship, naturally. Then we begin to think and become aware of God.

She continued,

I was in a kind of prison through agoraphobia for twenty-five years: there didn't seem a lot to be thankful for in those days. If you're released from a prison like that, or even turn the key yourself, you notice how blinded you've been to all the wonderful things and the goodness that you now see in people. Now I am constantly looking for God in people, believing him to be there, and believing that this God that I have discovered, who is love, who is kindness, who is gentleness, is speaking to me through them. He is there through them, and in his created world. And so, for me, the thankfulness thing goes on bubbling. It is the joy of freedom.

In the New Testament there are many references to offering our prayers with thanksgiving. Even when we are not naturally moved to do so, it is right to give thanksgiving a foremost place in our prayers. It is a way of showing our dependence upon God for everything and our sense that he is good and worthy to be thanked. It is the experience of many who pray that plenty of thanksgiving makes the journey lighter. It is as if God waits for us to acknowledge his goodness before he allows us to know that we are experiencing it. He looks for faith; and when we believe him to be as he is, the experience follows. Thanksgiving is a witness to the good gifts of God. The more we do it, the more the good gifts seem to come, and our whole attitude to life becomes more positive. It is an excellent pathway for prayer.

Prayer for Others

Prayer for others is another vital focus for words in prayer. Again Grace had a remarkable experience to share. This time it was about how difficult she found it to pray when she had her breakdown and how God began to resolve this for her.

I couldn't get the words right because nothing seemed to make any difference. It was something that David and I were reading together in Job that made the difference. It said, 'The Lord turned the captivity of Job when he prayed for his friends' (Job 42:10). So I entered into a sort of mechanical way of praying. David joined me in this. We were at the Mayflower Family Centre at the time and there was a list of church members, well over a hundred, and we tried to recall each of the members in a list, and I prayed for them one by one. It took the attention away from myself; it helped me to look beyond myself and to attend to those different individual people, all of whom I knew well. I would try and attend to their situation as well as I knew it, and, somehow, by attending to them in this way, that brought me the will to get better.

So the Lord turned the captivity of Job when he prayed for his friends, and he did that for me as well. It was something I wanted to do; it started off as a mechanical prayer list, but it turned out to be a company of sinners, a company of saints, a company of people; and it stopped me feeling so alone, as well.

27

It is hard to find a way of interceding for others that does not fall into routine, so that at times our prayers lack both compassion and conviction. One secret is to make sure that we are always seizing the initiative and changing our ways of praying in order to keep our motivation alive. To pray in the way that our heart inclines to is good advice, provided, of course, that it inclines to pray at all!

Many people use lists of people for different days of the week, but these can become lifeless. They then need to be changed or dropped altogether. To pray spontaneously is good, but self-discipline in organising ourselves to remember all those about whom we care is also good. Grace shared her experience.

I used to live on prayer lists as a student. I used to have lists and lists of Monday people, Tuesday people, Wednesday people. I know some people still do that. I meet people who pray for us on one of those days and it is very moving when you meet someone who says, 'We were praying for you today'. But I'm not very disciplined, and quite impulsive in my intercessory prayer. We meet so many people with needs. That's why the Anglican rites are helpful because they help you to focus on various sections.

I find that it's easier to pray for people who have special need. First, I try to picture the person, which is back to the stillness thing, again. I'm thinking now of someone who has been imprisoned recently after a very painful trial, and his family, and I try to enter into the pain of that with them. I stand with them in the prison. I stand with them in the home. I try to stand with them in the communities where people talk about them. I don't know what I say. I don't think God hears us for our much speaking, but he has given us the gift of words, and if we don't use it we are neglecting the gifts he has given us.

Praying Together

We can pray out loud, or we can pray silently, with the words in our thoughts. We can pray on our own, or we can pray together. Jesus promised that when two or three met together, in his name, he would be there with them. He declared that if two of his followers agreed together about anything that they would ask God the Father, it would be granted to them (Matthew 18:19–20). Sadly, we do not always give full value to these wonderful statements. At the least, however, they commend the value of learning to pray together. It can be done silently, but with an agreed intention. Alternatively, there is great value in learning to pray simple, spontaneous prayers out loud, in which the others present can share. My wife, Molly, and I pray like this both in the morning, and at bedtime. We use lists, and find it helpful to remember a variety of people over the course of a month.

The Roman Catholic Archbishop of Liverpool, Derek Worlock, was a close friend of the Sheppards. Grace drew my attention to papers of his, published shortly after his death, in which he spoke of how important it had been for his own spiritual growth to learn to pray out loud with others in an open way. This kind of shared prayer is not so usual in the more catholic traditions of Roman and Anglican Churches, and the Archbishop's testimony is, therefore, striking. The benefits which come from such openness in prayer come because to pray aloud in words is to allow other people to see something of our inner spiritual world. While this may be why we hesitate to do it, to share in this way is part of what is meant by the 'fellowship of the Holy Spirit'. Literally, this means the life of the Spirit which is shared or held in common. The more that is held in common, or the more agreement there is, the more the promise of Jesus that the Father will answer us can be fulfilled.

Another strong advocate of learning to pray out loud is the well-known Roman Catholic, Francis Macnutt. In a delightful short book, *The Prayer That Heals*, he urges married couples to learn to pray together. Apart from the joy it brings to pray on a daily basis it is important also so that they know what to do when someone in the family is ill. Macnutt has questioned many Christian congregations and found that only 20% of people were ever prayed with by their mothers and only 3% by their fathers. This is sad. The foundations of Christian teaching and prayer must be laid in our homes, with open commitment to a way of life in which prayer is central. It may be that the failure to do this is one of the reasons why basic Christian beliefs are being discarded by so many in Western society. Christians have not lived them as if they were the essential truth of life, a living relationship with the God who is at the heart of all things.

Writing our Prayers

As well as being spoken to God, words of prayer can be written. Cardinal Hume mentioned that he found it helpful to write prayers, and Grace Sheppard said the same. With words going round in her head she finds it helpful sometimes to write something down. The day we met was in the middle of a particularly busy time for her, and she was aware of the special needs of friends which have already been mentioned. This is the prayer that she had written the day before we met. She saw it as a kind of psalm.

Lord, this is a busy patch.
It's hard to sit still.
My thoughts wander.

I need to make lists to make sense of today's tasks.
Sickness, disability, old age and death are
  surrounding us.
Even crime has stalked us, with friends facing court
  and imprisonment.

Will the centre hold?
So much seems to depend on me.
But then I remember that I am not the centre.
So I relax a little.

You are the centre.
I look to the centre.
I look to you.
I depend on you.
I know you are there in the eye of the storm: calm
  unphased, and with gentle power.

Be with those who are facing suffering and
  uncertainty; especially . . .
  calm their storm.

Be with those who have lost a loved one, suddenly;
  especially . . .
  calm their storm.

Be with those whose bodies have seized up with
  arthritis; especially . . .
  calm their storm.

'Peace, be still.'
I am still now. I am ready for the day.

The different categories in the prayer refer to different
people, Grace explained. Writing this down helps her to
intercede. Having written the prayer she explained that
it would stay in her notebook, somewhere in her room,
and she would use it again, perhaps in the evening.

31

Perhaps it is all very well to speak of prayer as about being natural, and flowing between the use of words and silence, and into and out of the use of other senses. For those who are trying to get to get grips with the life of prayer something clear and specific can be very helpful. So I asked Grace what she would say to someone who was learning to pray about what words to use.

> There are several things I would want to say. One of them is this: 'Just sit quietly. You don't have to use words if you don't want to. You don't have to be good at words to pray. Just be with God.'
>
> If they find that disturbing, I would tell them to think of a warm shower, or of the sun (as I have described it), and let that be God's acceptance to them, something that makes them feel comfortable with themselves. And then, stop and listen; or stop and handle (as with the lavender). Let God be God. Then the words will come.

What about a restless person, I asked, who would find it hard to pray just by being with God?

> I would say, 'You carry on being restless, and be restless with God. He's not going to tick you off for being restless. Neither will he desert you.'

Grace referred to the book *Just as I Am*, by Ruth Etchells, and quoted Ruth's experience:

> 'I find that my thoughts flitter about, that I embrace distraction and that sometimes it is with the utmost difficulty that I can make myself even begin.'

And for the person who can't find the right words?

> Tell God about it. Just say 'I can't find the right words.' But talk to him.

There are no right words. There are no wrong words. Once one becomes aware that we are accepted as we are, warts and all, it's like a small child walking, like me walking with my father, which I cannot remember, sadly. I can walk with him now, in his eighty-sixth year, and say quite naturally to him, 'I feel all over the place'. He is not going to start slapping me down and saying, 'Pull yourself together', or 'You shouldn't be like that'. He just goes on walking alongside me.

The Lord's Prayer

As we seek to build good patterns of daily prayer into our lives we have been given wonderful resources of words to use. The most universally used prayer is the Lord's Prayer. Here, from Jesus himself, we have simple words to use in prayer. We also have a pattern around which to shape our prayers. It can be seen as having 6 points.

1. Prayer of opening address to God, with intimacy and reverence.
   Our Father, who art in heaven,
   hallowed be thy Name;
2. Prayer for the earth to be as God wants, for people to let him have his way in their lives.
   thy kingdom come;
   thy will be done; on earth as it is in heaven.
3. Prayer for God to provide for our daily needs, and those of his world.
   Give us this day our daily bread.
4. Prayer for God to forgive the wrong we do.
   And forgive us our trespasses, as we forgive those
   who trespass against us.
5. Prayer for God to protect us from evil.

And lead us not into temptation;
but deliver us from evil.
6. Concluding prayer of praise.
    For thine is the kingdom, the power and the glory,
    for ever and ever. Amen.

It is helpful, as the prayer is said, to focus on one of
these 6 points so that saying the familiar words does not
simply become a routine.

Grace explained what she found helpful about the
Lord's Prayer.

> It's always alive! It always has meaning for today, for
> now. The fact that it starts off with 'Our Father' gives
> me a sense that I'm part of a very large family and
> that I'm not alone. It seems to have everything there.
> I can remember a time when I was badly out of sorts
> with somebody. I didn't feel like forgiving them at
> all. And yet, day after day, week after week, we say
> the Lord's Prayer where we ask him to forgive us
> in the way we forgive other people. There was a log
> jam there for me, personally, both with the person I
> am talking about and with God. There was no
> moving forward because I didn't want to forgive;
> and yet the thought of not being forgiven by God
> in the way that I wasn't forgiving this person
> was almost intolerable. So it has a daily challenge
> there for everyday relationships; and I did even-
> tually get to the point when I put it right with
> this person and was able to forgive, and also to say
> sorry.

Grace went on to say how the prayer helped her to keep
a sense of transcendence when the household chores
were making everything feel very earthy.

> When you are taken up with a lot of nitty gritty
> busyness in this earthy world, like in my case at
> the moment, it means doing a lot of entertaining,

cleaning, cooking, while at the same time trying to appear cool and calm and collected, remembering that God's presence is always in the background lifts my eyes above all that. There is another world beside my busy world and that actually helps me to get a sense of proportion. 'Our Father, who art in heaven . . .': where is heaven? It is both here and beyond, especially when the busy patch doesn't feel very much like heaven. It lifts me out of myself; so that gives a transcendence. I think it is important to be able to be in this world with our feet on the ground, with all the things we have to attend to, but also to take wing sometimes and be above it, and see it in perspective.

Other Resources

The other great area of written resources is found in the liturgical prayer books produced by most Churches, and in books of prayers, both contemporary and past. Grace's grandfather, a clergyman, often quoted the collects, the prayers for each week of the Church's year. At the time she thought this was a bit boring, but now she values such prayers. People used to learn collects by heart and Grace can recite a few. She also remembers being made to learn two psalms at school, as a punishment. While she didn't think that using the Bible as a punishment was appropriate, she found that when she was ill in hospital she was very thankful to have them firmly lodged in her memory, as a prayer. Storing rich prayers of Scripture and tradition like this gives us resources to draw on when we need the words of others for our prayers.

Grace highlighted one such prayer from *Celebrating Common Prayer*, set for reading after saying Psalm 148. We close this chapter with it.

O glorious God,
the whole of creation proclaims your marvellous
   work:
increase in us a capacity to wonder and delight in it,
that heaven's praise may echo in our hearts
and our lives be spent as good stewards of the earth;
through Jesus Christ our Lord. Amen.

GROUP STUDY

*Share something of how your prayer has been in the past
week. How has it been different from the previous week's
prayer? Share any difficulties as well as the things you
have found helpful.*

 We communicate in many different ways with
people. We may let them know what we feel
and think by a look, a gesture, a touch, a grunt,
or by silence, but very often we use words. In the group,
briefly discuss why it is that we use words so much.

Praying through words is an integral part of Christian
tradition. Many of us learned to say prayers as children.
As we grow in our use of language, so we can grow in
our use of prayers.

There are times when we find that our prayers take us
beyond words, there are other times when words are
essential. Many people know the experience of wanting
to pray, but not knowing what to say. Sometimes we find
that the way prayers are worded in church does not help
us to express our own feelings to God.

Using our own words

 Going round the group, list the different ways
in which you talk to God. What sort of things
do you talk about? What kinds of things do
you say?

There is no need to discuss these – simply make a list, allowing everyone in the group to make a contribution, however brief. Then see how the items on your list fall into these different ways of talking to God.

saying sorry	being angry
complaining	thinking things through
talking things over	saying thank you
asking for things	expressing love

On your own, in silence, reflect on which of these you do most often and which you do least often.

If you are using the cassette tape, listen to the interview with Grace Sheppard.

In the group, discuss the advantages of using your own words to pray. Share your experiences of conversational prayer (see p.22–5) and of family prayer (see pp.29, 30).

Using other people's words
Words can sometimes fail us when we are trying to pray. It is then that other people's prayers can come to our rescue. Below there are different ways that we can use the words of others in prayer: using a 'daily office' from a prayer book or using the Lord's Prayer.

Something to read
An important part of Christian tradition for many people is sharing in the prayers of the worldwide Church in a simple rhythm of daily prayer.

This can be done by using an established form of words which does not vary with our changing moods.

There are many different forms of daily prayer available. In the Anglican tradition there are the services of

Morning and Evening Prayer in the *Book of Common Prayer*, *The Alternative Service Book* (which offers a longer, and a shorter, form) and a recent publication called *Celebrating Common Prayer*. Other Churches have their own patterns of regular liturgical prayer.

When using one of these forms of prayer, even if we are alone, there is a very real sense that we are part of the Church's prayer throughout the world. The knowledge that there are other people in other places, using exactly the same prayers, makes us aware of being part of the Communion of Saints in which those who have gone before us join their prayers with ours as part of the worship of heaven.

 In pairs, discuss briefly your own experience of a regular form of daily prayer and what you found helpful or unhelpful. If you have never experienced this form of prayer, say what you like or dislike about the idea.

When Jesus' disciples asked him to teach them to pray, he taught them a prayer. The prayer he taught them was the one that we know as the 'Lord's Prayer'. The version that we normally use can be found in **Matthew 6:9–13**. Read the other version of this prayer from **Luke 11:1–4**.

 We use the Lord's Prayer both as a model of what to include in our praying and also as a prayer whose words we actually say.

Grace Sheppard said of the Lord's Prayer, 'It's always alive! It always has meaning for today, for now' (p. 34). She spoke of her experience of being challenged and lifted by the prayer.

Discuss what you find helpful or unhelpful about this prayer.

Your own experience

In groups of two or three share, in detail, with one another the ways in which you use words in your prayers. Do you mostly use your own words or other people's? Which books of prayers do you find most helpful? Do you sometimes use the words of hymns or songs? Do you ever write down your prayers or make a note of the things you have prayed about?

Share any points that stood out for you from the experiences of Grace Sheppard.

In the same small groups, produce some key guidelines, about using words in prayer, that you would want to pass on to someone who is just beginning to pray. If there is time, let each small group share their guidelines with the whole group and discuss them together.

In a time of prayer, let each person write down a short prayer of only one or two sentences. Then let everyone read their prayer, in turn, around the room. Alternatively, have a few minutes of open prayer in which anyone can say their own prayer or recite a prayer that they have learned.

End the meeting by saying the Lord's Prayer together, slowly.

DURING THE WEEK

On each day of the coming week do one of the following.

• Many Old Testament characters have opened their hearts to God after an important moment in their lives. Look up one of the passages below and think how this prayer can enrich and inspire your own

prayers. In the light of these thoughts, write a prayer
that arises from your own life.

Exodus 14:26–15:21   **Nehemiah 1**   **Jonah 2**

- Thank God for everything that has been good about
  the last few days.
- Write a letter to God, telling him, honestly, how you
  are feeling about your life at present. You may like
  to keep the letter, simply throw it away, or burn it as
  a sign of offering it to God.
- Bring to God anything that is on your conscience or
  getting in the way of your relationship with him.
  Say 'sorry' and anything else that you wish to say
  about it.
- Use a form of 'Daily Office' on your own; alternatively join Morning Prayer, Evening Prayer or the
  daily Eucharist at your church or one near your
  place of work.
- Choose a psalm (perhaps one from p. 58) and read
  through it slowly, entering into it as your own
  prayer.
- Read the next chapter of this book, 'Praying
  through Scripture'.

Session 3

Praying through Scripture

with Donald English

To travel the pathways of prayer we need direction. We need to hear God's voice. The journey is about coming home to him, and he must direct us there. The voice of God is not an audible voice, but the unmistakeable sense that he is calling us and guiding us.

The voice of God addresses us supremely through Holy Scripture. It is 'the word of the Lord'. God has not only acted powerfully to rescue his world, he wants us to interpret these acts correctly. So he has spoken to us his interpretation of his acts in the Scriptures, and he continues to speak through them today. The most important thing, then, about praying through Scripture is that we let God speak to us. In handling the Bible we are opening ourselves to the voice of God, and it has great power to change us.

Donald English was until recently the chairman of the World Methodist Council, and is well known in English Free Church circles. He has twice been President of the Methodist Conference, and is also a former Moderator of the Free Church Federal Council. We met in the living room of his home in the Cotswolds.

A Glimpse into the Control Room

Donald shared how the Scriptures find a place in his prayers.

> I learned right at the beginning of my Christian life that praying and reading Scriptures go together. So, in that sense, the Scriptures form the framework within which I pray. I think the most important thing is the picture which the Scripture gives of God in relation to the world, establishing him to be the God of all the worlds there are. I am constantly reminded by Scripture that I am coming into the presence of the one who is Lord of all, and that the focal point is him and not me.

If God is central to all that is going on in the world, then the Scriptures take us into his control room where 'the voice of God' introduces us to something of the way things are in his world. But, if God is at the centre of everything, why is he interested at all in our prayers? Donald explained this using a model which shed more light on the sense of partnership.

> It seems to me that the creation of the world is the extension of the life of God, Father, Son and Holy Spirit, to include, lovingly, everything that he has made. And within that context there is a freedom of relationship where God has, if I may so put it, a vision for how the world is and how it should be. But it isn't set in concrete, it is established as things develop. We play our part and we make our contribution. I think our praying is rather like the father of a family allowing all the members of the family to play their part in conversation as to how the family should be run.

It is a strange thing, this prayer! For God knows perfectly well what we all need. But prayer is not, primarily, about what we need. It is about being drawn into the way God wants his world to be. If we stop to think about it, how else could we join in God's great work to heal the world? God is invisible. We cannot see him. Yet, somehow, we must relate to him. It is prayer that gathers us in. Prayer is the conversation, and more. It is the pulling of our hearts and minds into line with God. He interacts with our sense of responsibility but he does not override it. He is trying to make us true adults, who know that our well-being is in him and who choose accordingly. So he calls us to be *in partnership* with him. Prayer opens up the partnership.

Donald described Leslie Weatherhead's image of the tapestry to illustrate the patient way in which God is working with human beings in spite of our failures.

You look at the front of the tapestry and it all looks very neat and tidy, but when you go round the back you see all the broken bits that are tied in, that have been somehow worked into the pattern. I think that's how Scripture teaches us the way in which God operates in the world; from the beginning with the creation, to the very end and the triumph of Revelation. Between these two, God is at work lovingly in the world, calling people to serve with him, to work with him, to discern his will and to play their part in making that will come about.

Only from the Scriptures can we begin to grasp the great world purposes into which God is calling us. Our hearing and responding to the voice of God in prayer will be formed by our reading of the Bible.

Together, we thought about how particular insights from Scripture might shape our prayers. For Donald, there is the fact that our God has worldwide concerns.

When I come to say my prayers, I am not coming only about the question of myself, my wife and my home and my children, and so on. It's the question of how God sees the whole world. Therefore, the pressure on the praying is to pray not only for that which is going on here in this village, but also what is happening in Israel and what is happening in South Africa and what is happening elsewhere – because that is the God I am praying to, and those are his concerns.

In the last chapter we observed how the Lord's Prayer taught us to pray for God's will on earth, that is, his worldwide Kingdom, the time when he will have his way. The overwhelming message of Scripture is of a God who has very loving purposes for his world, and is longing for us to share this mission with him.

Donald applies his world perspective to the way he

45

reads the Bible and the prayers that flow out of his reading. For example, with the parables of Jesus.

I have only quite lately in my life begun to say to myself in my praying, 'Lord, what does this parable mean for those who never hear it? What does the parable of the Prodigal Son mean for those who don't come to church, and who don't apply it individually?' And I suddenly began to realise that corporations are prodigal. That is, the prodigal son took the father's wealth and imagined that it was now his and squandered it. Corporations can be prodigal with the Father's good things. Nations can be prodigal with what they have had put into their possession, internationally. You start with where it affects you personally, saying, 'Lord, I've wasted what you gave to me, please take me back.' Then I find myself welcomed into the party and part of the family, again. But our prayers should never be allowed just to stay individualistic. They need to keep on spreading out. The moment you say about the teaching of Jesus, 'What has that to say in my world today?', you begin to discover areas of his meaning that we have not seen before.

I found it a challenging thought that I might pray for great world corporations or nations to 'come to themselves', to turn around, and no longer to throw away what God the Father has given them. It is, after all, not theirs but his. (The parable is in Luke 15.)

The Bible also insists that at the centre of the world's control room, so to speak, is Jesus Christ. It is he who holds everything together in the control room. He is the centre of God's purposes, the one who unites everything. Donald finds that the Scriptures about Christ give enormous content to his prayers. I asked him if he has any favourite Scriptures that are often part of his prayers. He took me straight to John, chapter 1.

46

'In the beginning was the Word and the Word was with God. The same was in the beginning with God. All things were made through him and without him was not anything made that was made . . . The Word became flesh and dwelt among us.'

That seems to me to be saying that the one who died for us on the cross is the heartbeat of the entire created universe. So when I say my prayers *in the name of Jesus*, I am saying my prayers in the name of the one, who, as the Word from the beginning, is the centre of everything that is. Therefore, I deeply believe, and it is the centre of my prayers, that the world will only work when it works according to that which God revealed in Jesus.

Here is another very helpful idea for our own prayers, that we might pray for everything to come together according to the pattern made known in Jesus, and held by him in complete unity.

St John's use of 'the Word' as the title for Jesus has important Hebrew and Greek links. It links with the Hebrew idea of the powerful word or voice of God. When God speaks, things always happen. Jesus, therefore, is God's commanding voice. The Greeks, on the other hand, saw 'the Word' as the great rational principle which held everything together and prevented disintegration and chaos. The 'word' gives coherence. In calling Jesus 'the Word', St John boldly asserts that the one who was sent from heaven to earth and became a man for us, is also the one in whom God's cosmic purposes hold together. Jesus is the one through whom what God has planned for the whole universe will be accomplished. This is a daring claim, but it is what God says to us.

Praying through Scripture, then, we see the world through the eyes of God. We cry out that the people of the world might find their peace in Jesus. We cry out for all things to come to their coherence in Jesus, the environment and the whole universe, that everything might find in Jesus its unity and its peace.

The Sweet Words of Love

In the study at the end of this chapter one of the exercises invites us to take the words of Scripture as a personal message to us about our place in God's design. We are to read them very carefully and slowly, just as we would a love letter. Or, we are to take them as a sweet to suck for the flavour and the enjoyment. The psalmist used similar thoughts:

> Your promise, how sweet to my palate!
> Sweeter than honey to my mouth!
>
> (Psalms 119:103)

There is a well-known Benedictine tradition in which the slow reading of Scripture is an encounter with God. If we say a phrase of Scripture slowly and meditatively, it opens the way for God to speak. It is helpful to sit upright and still, to relax all the body muscles, to breathe deeply and begin by handing over to God all the everyday cares which crowd into our thoughts. Then we repeat slowly the same text, for example, 'Be still, and know that I am God', or 'I am the Good Shepherd; I lay down my life for my sheep'. If this is followed by a period of silence, rich encounters with God may continue; they may lead into our offering ourselves or bringing the needs of others to him in prayer.

It can be helpful to learn Scriptures that describe God, and pray them over, slowly. One of my favourites is:

> 'The Lord, the Lord, a God merciful and gracious, slow to anger, and abounding in steadfast love and

faithfulness, keeping steadfast love for thousands, forgiving iniquity and transgression and sin.'

(Exodus 34: 6–7)

Donald spoke of 'the lovely passage in Deuteronomy' where the message to the people is:

'If Yahweh set his heart on you and chose you, it was not because you outnumbered other peoples . . . it was for love of you.'

(Deuteronomy 7:7)

He went on to mention

. . . this lovely sense that God loves them because he loves them. I find myself caught up in that again and again, in the idea that the love of God does not need a reason. God is love and therefore he loves.

Of course, there is a drawback to the imagery of the love letter and the sweet: both are rather self-orientated, self-indulgent pictures. Donald was quick to balance them by saying that while God may very much wish to speak to us of his love for us, his love is expressed in the cross of Jesus, and leads us to look outwards as well as inwards.

I think the message is, to quote from a Charles Wesley hymn: 'For all my Lord was crucified; for all, for all my Saviour died.' 'I love you and am glad you love me; and wouldn't it be wonderful if we could spread this love to everybody else?' So it's a letter which expresses love from the Father to his children in a way which so reveals his heart of love that the children dare not say, 'Let's suck that sweetie a little longer', but rather, 'He wants everybody. How are we going to communicate that to others?' Neither love letter, nor sweetie to be sucked, quite says that to me.

Donald described his way of using the Bible in his prayers as a process of first understanding what the Scripture is saying and then expressing in his own words the understanding he has received. This is the sense in which the Scriptures are a map for his prayers. It is as if he says, 'If this is the direction to go, I will follow it in my prayers'. If, for example, he has read the words of Jesus about losing your life to find it, and he then considers the day ahead of him, he might pray like this:

> 'Lord, I thank you that I have read again what I have known for a long time, that it is by offering my life in the service of you and others that I will have possession of it. Now I look through today and see where are the moments when it is likely that these challenges are going to be made of me'. I will try to be specific about what it is I am going to do today, who I am going to meet today, and what it will mean in that situation to give myself.

The immediate example that sprang to Donald's mind, from his pre-retirement days, was difficult committees! (I assured him that if he had a good Scripture for such occasions this would sell a lot of books!) He went on to explain how the prayer of self-giving might work out.

> I think I would say, 'Lord, I understand that David today will want a large amount of the money for the social and political concerns which are his responsibility. I understand that John's concern for training of the ministers means he has to battle for the resources there. My concern is for the mission of the Methodist Church in the world. Lord, help us to give ourselves enough to be hearing one another. Help us each to understand one another's point of view and then help us each, in self-giving, to discover

what the way forward is which you, yourself, supremely have.'

Now that would be the way the prayer would work out; and that's a very nitty gritty thing, which puts you into a very difficult situation when you go into the committee room, because you are already committed to understanding and helping the others to do what they want to do. And that's the way of the cross. I think it's that lowly, suffering, self-giving love which is raised from the dead; and Christian leaders find that very hard because each has a clientele looking to them to argue their case and provide for their needs.

The voice of God through the Scriptures calls us into specific action, often making us the answer to our own prayers. There are biblical characters like Samuel and Nehemiah who offer themselves to God and then find that, in a particular situation, they become the answer to their own prayers. In a similar way, as we identify with the people of faith in the Bible, and pray in the light of what we read, we find that God has also put his hand on us for a particular task. As Donald noted:

So often in the Bible people go to God and say, 'You know, there's a problem here!' And God says, 'Well, what about you?' Nehemiah goes to God in prayer and says, 'The city has broken down; it's terrible, and your Name is being disregarded.' God says, 'How much time have you got? Why don't you ask for leave and go and do something about it?' Now the biblical stories are meant to affect our praying in that way. They provide content to the praying, and possibilities within the praying, of ourselves becoming the answers to the prayers we are saying.

The Mirror

Home is a place where we are faced with ourselves. Those closest to us, because they love us, will help us to see ourselves as we really are. Then we can address the need to change. The voice of God, similarly, is a voice which faces us with ourselves that we might admit our wrong, receive God's word of forgiveness, and allow ourselves to be changed. There is no question that God always accepts us as we are. His voice about our faults is only that we might live in the truth with both a godly sorrow that this is the way we are and a holy joy that all is truly forgiven.

Donald English put it like this:

> It is very difficult to touch many places in Scripture where you don't suddenly find yourself looking into a mirror, which causes you to say, 'My word, yes, I do understand. I don't do exactly what David did; I don't do what this one did, or that one, but I can see a pretty good parallel there.' You look at the disciples and you say, 'Oh! Why didn't they understand it?' And then you suddenly feel, 'How much do I actually understand what is going on?' So, I think the biblical material is constantly holding up a mirror to our faces. We see in the mirror, as Paul put it in 2 Corinthians 3 [v. 18], not our faces reflected in the mirror, but his love for us reflected in the mirror. But the effect of that is to cause us to say, 'Is that who I am?' So, all of that is at work all through the biblical story, from the Fall right through to the End. It is the struggle of individuals who find themselves out of harmony with God's way, but also offered a chance to be in harmony.

Pressed a little further about how he might pray when the Bible had faced him with one of his sins or failings, Donald said that his prayer might go like this,

'Lord, there I go again. I keep on meaning to get that right and I don't get it right. I thank you that, again, I dare to come in the Name of Jesus and know that there is forgiveness for the penitent; and I ask not only to be forgiven, but to be helped, by the power of your Spirit, to move forward to better ways of living my life in that area.'

The Arrows

There are many times when a sentence of Scripture is ready to hand as the ideal prayer, right on target, so to speak. One of the most well known is the Jesus Prayer, originally developed in the Orthodox Church, but now widely used all over the world.

'Lord Jesus Christ, Son of God, have mercy upon me, a sinner.'

The biblical origin of this prayer will be obvious in the Gospels. In one of Jesus' parables, he describes two people praying. It was the rogue, the tax-collector, and not the proud religious leader, who prayed the prayer acceptable to God, 'God, be merciful to me, a sinner' (Luke 18:13).

On another occasion, a blind beggar called out, 'Jesus, Son of David, have mercy on me!' (Luke 18:39). People tried to silence him, but he was heard by Jesus and received his sight. The Jesus Prayer weaves the two together. Its simplest form is, 'Lord Jesus Christ, have mercy upon me.' With the most remarkable simplicity, the prayer declares the true identity of Jesus, and acknowledges total dependence upon his pardon, his healing and his power to carry us forward. It expresses the right way to live daily, before God.

The traditional use of the prayer is to repeat it many times. It then becomes part of us. It is recalled instinctively at any time in the day or night. When repeated many times, in a strange way, it seems that the Spirit begins to pray it in us. It is pure Gospel.

Donald shared a different example of a phrase of Scripture ready to hand, the cry of Jesus on the cross.

> Sometimes for others I found myself shouting out, 'My God, my God, why have you forsaken – them?' [Mark 15:34, replacing 'me' with 'them'.]
>
> I think of a little child dying of bone cancer, a little three-year-old, and having to conduct the service. And, it wasn't happening to me, but I felt the sort of desertedness of that, and preached on that at the service.

Rather than follow exactly the words of Scripture, Donald finds it more helpful to put what the Scripture is saying into his own words for prayer.

> I find that it is much better to read the Scripture, understand what the Scripture is saying, and then try to turn it into my own language, so that the passage of Scripture becomes, if I may put it like this, mine in this situation. And I try to translate it into this context. So, the same loving God, the same dying and rising Jesus, the same powerful Holy Spirit, and the same Scripture is the reality; but I am saying how it becomes true for me.

Taking a further example, Donald makes the familiar words about Jesus emptying himself the basis for a prayer for Northern Ireland.

> What shall we pray for Ireland? What we need for Ireland is more leaders who are willing to go the way of lowly, suffering love and to risk themselves in the face of their own supporters as De Klerk and Mandela did in South Africa. For that is the way, to have leaders who are willing enough to risk them-

selves to say, 'Whatever my supporters are saying, in the interests of peace, I'll go this step, whatever it costs me.' That's Philippians 2: 'Who, though he was equal with God, thought not equality with God a thing to be grasped at, but humbled himself, became obedient, even to death, death on a cross. Wherefore, God has lifted him up. . . .'

That's a kind of parabola from glory to glory, via lowly suffering love, which for me is the pattern for living, and, therefore, for praying.

Raw Human Emotions

No discussion of praying through Scripture would be complete without mention of the Psalms. Here, in particular, God is affirming the whole range of human emotions. There is great joy, and there is raw pain. All moods find their place in the Psalms. There is reflective wisdom, there are laments. There is poetry full of wonder at creation. There is recitation of the history of God's people, sometimes the positive strands, sometimes the negative. There is confession of sin. We are provided with a kind of God-given hymn-book with something to fit where we are. It is very reassuring. God has provided these Psalms in his revelation. This is his voice saying that he accepts us, poor and vulnerable, even twisted, as we are. As Cardinal Hume said, 'We need to make friends amongst the Psalms.' We cannot know them all. But with a bit of exploration and trial we can find the ones that speak for us, the ones that voice our pain, and the ones that lift us up.

Donald spoke about his use of the Psalms.

The Psalmist tells me day by day to have my feet on the ground and realise that life depends each day on God's graciousness to me. I may get up in the morning imagining that this is another day of life that is mine by right; but in reality it is a gift. This sheer vulnerable humanity and the constant crying out to God for the next day's life is something that our sophisticated world has forgotten about. So, I am just learning that now. I am having some medical treatment myself at the moment, so mortality suddenly becomes a kind of reality. When you go to the Psalms you discover that is how the Psalmist lived.

I asked Donald in more detail how he used a particular psalm. He told me that he studied a psalm to pick up its major lessons, its insights and feelings. Then, in the light of his forthcoming treatment, he shared a typical prayer.

'Lord, as the Psalmist knew his life depended on you day by day, so does mine. As the Psalmist called on you to protect and save him in need, so do I. As the Psalmist had to learn that sometimes things happen that he didn't plan and he didn't choose, so do I. So as the Psalmist's life was in your hands, literally, so I put my life into your hands, literally.'

Scripture, then, offers us a great many ways in which, on the one hand, we hear the voice of God, and on the other hand, we are provided with words and models for every kind of mood and situation, to take and use in our prayers. Prayer is a relationship with God, a partnership. He is the good companion and more. He is the centre of everything. Yet he cares about us. He seeks to draw out our responsibility. He calls us to choose to work with him and to pray the prayers which are closest to his will. He is always forming us along the way. He guides us to our true home.

This journey cannot be undertaken profitably without learning to hear the voice of God, which means listening and praying through Scripture. Let us take to heart the Psalmist's words for our pathways of prayer,

If only you would listen to him today,
'Do not harden your hearts.'

(Psalm 95:7)

GROUP STUDY

Take time to settle down. Perhaps use some quiet music. Relax, let the concerns of the day fade away. Be aware of your feelings as you await the evening and what God may have in store for you.

Have an open Bible in a prominent place – perhaps with a lighted candle.

 Share briefly something of what your prayer has meant for you over the past week – the difficulties as well as what you have found enriching.

If you are using the cassette tape, listen now to the interview with Donald English.

 In the group, share which of these approaches to the Scriptures described in this chapter is most natural for you to use as a key to your prayers.

The sense of being in God's control room
The sweet words of love
The map which guides
The mirror that shows us ourselves
The arrows that are ready-to-hand prayers
The expressions of raw human emotions

There is not time in this session to try all these approaches to prayer. That will have to be done at home or at another time. Here are four different ways of praying through Scripture: using the Psalms, sweet words of love, praying to God's pattern and imaginative contemplation on a Gospel story. There will probably only be time to do two of these.

1. Using the Psalms

Something to read

Jesus, when he was being crucified, spoke out the words of **Psalm 22**, 'My God, my God, why have you forsaken me?' Here was no moment for making his own prayers. It was at that moment that the prayers he had learned by heart many years ago came to his rescue.

The Bible is rich with prayers, often spoken at times of crisis and need. The book of Psalms contains many such prayers.

We can pour out our experience, e.g. in **Psalm 130** 'Out of the depths I cry out to you, O Lord . . .'

We can join with all creation in worshipping God, e.g. in **Psalm 148**. 'Praise him, all his angels, praise him, all you shining stars. Praise him, sun and moon, praise him, all you highest heavens, and you waters above the skies.'

We can celebrate with words the transformation that God is bringing in our lives, e.g. in **Psalm 103** 'He forgives all my sins and heals all my diseases; he redeems my life from the pit and crowns me with love and compassion. He satisfies my desires with good things so that my youth is renewed like the eagle's.'

We can enjoy the perspective that worshipping God gives to the rest of our lives, e.g. in **Psalm 92** 'The senseless man does not know, fools do not understand, that though the wicked spring up like grass and all evildoers flourish, they will be for ever destroyed. But you, O Lord, are exalted for ever.'

The prayers of others, learned by heart in calmer days, can come to our rescue in moments of need. Our emotions and concerns can be held in the rhythms of familiar words.

Our feelings can be reflected in the words of others who have grappled with the same problems and have expressed their thoughts with a beauty and simplicity we could never match, e.g. the prayer of Richard of Chichester at the end of session 1: '. . . to know you more clearly, love you more dearly and follow you more nearly. . . .'

 On your own, choose one of the passages quoted above and reflect upon it, repeating it and soaking it in. Choose the passage that is most appropriate to how you feel and let it nourish you.

 Read one of the Psalms above and try to grasp its main meaning. Take that meaning and put it into your own silent words of prayer, be it in praise of God, for yourself or for the good of the world.

As a group, review your experience of this prayer.

2. Sweet words of love

Something to read

The Bible is like a love letter from God to us, the creatures he made out of love to be his sons and daughters. You do not read a letter from a lover in a cursory way and then throw it away; you read and reread it, because it is so personal, so intimate.

At times you may read something which is difficult to accept. You may be thrilled by the sheer joy of a phrase.

The words written by someone who cares for you will be words you savour and ponder and treat with respect.

We should read the Bible like that. It is God telling us how much he loves us. If we can 'hear' that word of love and accept it, we will want to respond to that love. So we need to read the Bible slowly, prayerfully and expectantly.

This slow, ruminating way of using Scripture is deep in the Christian tradition. As we saw earlier this is especially a Benedictine way of prayer. The followers of St Benedict would read a passage very slowly and stop whenever a word or phrase spoke to them. They stayed with it, savouring it, speaking to the Lord about what it was saying to them. Or they would just rest in what they had been given.

It can be helpful to mouth the words, to pause at the end of a phrase, going over it again and again until it sinks in – like sucking a sweet until it is totally absorbed.

If we were brought up in the Church, the Scriptures can be over-familiar to us, so that we no longer hear their dynamic message. Remember, you are not just reading an ordinary book. You are meeting a person, God himself.

When something strikes you, or when you feel moved or challenged, speak to the Lord about what you feel, as one friend speaks to another.

∾∾

 Have a time of silent prayer using *one* of the following passages. Read it slowly, perhaps a number of times. As another saint, Ignatius of Loyola, said, 'What fills and satisfies the soul is not knowing much, but in understanding the realities profoundly and in savouring them interiorly.' So always stay with what 'fills and satisfies' you. There is no need to get to the end of a passage. Stay with the word that echoes in your heart, however faintly.

Luke 12:22–31   **Psalm 62**
Romans 8:28–39   **Jeremiah 29:11–14**

 Share as much as you want to of what that time of prayer meant to you.

 In the full group, share again. Listen to what is being said. God may speak again to you through someone else's prayer experience. It is not helpful to discuss or question what other people say. Just listen and accept.

3. Praying to God's pattern

 In the group, read one of the following passages of Scripture

John 1:1–5   **Luke 15:17–24**
Philippians 2:4–11   **Colossians 1:15–20**

Allow time to reflect on the passage. What basis does it show for praying for God's ways to come in the world, or in specific situations?

Either pray in silence or in short simple prayers out loud in the group.

This exercise can be repeated using a different passage.

4. Imaginative contemplation on a Gospel story

<hr>

Something to read

When you are reading a novel by a favourite author which absorbs you, your feelings are aroused, your imagination creates the scene and you are lost in the story.

There are many narratives in the Bible which we can read in this way. Whether they are real happenings or stories told, we can take time to get into the scene, give our imagination full play, allow the spirit of the story to arouse us.

We may find we are an observer, or one of the characters. In this way the person of Jesus can come alive for us and we can feel the emotions and enter into the experiences of the characters in the story.

This is a kind of prayer in which the imagination and emotions are involved as well as the mind, and so we can be affected more deeply.

We cannot rush this kind of prayer. It takes time to absorb the atmosphere.

 Try this method now, using the story of the stilling of the storm in **Luke 8:22–5**. Imagine the buffeting of the wind; the cold soaking from the waves crashing onto the boat. Discover the rising panic of the disciples as their boat sinks lower and lower into the water. Experience the presence of Jesus as he deals with the situation.

The text for this exercise is printed in the back of this book on p. 113. The leader can use this to lead the contemplation for the whole group. The contemplation is also recorded on the cassette tape that accompanies the book. If using the tape, when everyone is ready, simply turn the tape to the beginning of side two and play it.

Talk over what this has meant to you. Be careful to listen to other people without commenting or questioning.

DURING THE WEEK

Here are some suggestions. You may not have time for them all. Use those you feel drawn to.

- Try the parts of the exercises that you did not use during the group meeting.
- Pray through one or more of the following passages.

    Put your name in the text where it says *Israel, Jacob* or *Ephraim*.

Isaiah 41:8–14	**Isaiah 43:1–3**
Hosea 11:1–4 & 8–9	**Jeremiah 1:4–8**

    Hear God speaking the words to *you*. They are to you as much as to the original writer or anyone else. Pause after each phrase. Repeat the words again and again.

- Take part of the prayer of Jesus for his followers in John 17:6–11 and 15–26. Think of him praying for you. Speak the words out loud, or mouth them silently. Put your own name in and change the wording to personalise it, *e.g.* '*I have made your name known to Beryl/Brian. . . .*'
- You could use one or more of the following Gospel stories in an imaginative prayer as outlined in no. 4, Imaginative contemplation

    Mark 5:25–34   **Luke 19:1–10**   **John 5:1–9**

- Read chapter 4 of this book, 'Praying through Silence'.

Session 4

Praying through Silence
with Gerard W. Hughes

In a world full of noise, more and more people are searching for silence, silence in which to find peace, silence in which to get in touch with themselves and with God. Throughout the centuries, the masters of prayer have taught the central place of silence in the journey with God. Today, it is striking that Christians of very varied Church traditions are coming together in exploring their common desire to learn the prayer of silence.

Gerry Hughes is a Jesuit priest, well known for the training courses he has established on the art of spiritual direction, and for his book *God of Surprises*. We met in Manresa House, in the suburbs of Birmingham, the Jesuit house in Harborne where Gerry lives. Our conversation began with the importance of silence. Gerry drew an immediate distinction between outer silence, that is, the silence of the surroundings, and inner silence, the silence inside ourselves.

Silence in the Surroundings

Reflecting on silence in the surroundings, we concluded that it cannot be an absolute essential for prayer, otherwise people in cities have no chance. However, Gerry explained the importance of outer silence like this.

It is because it is conducive to the inner silence. The outer silence enables us to get far more in touch with what is happening *inside*. In all of us there is far more going on than our conscious minds can grasp, and what is going on is often in our subconscious or unconscious, and yet it is influencing the way we see reality, and the way we act, the way we react. And, consequently, we find life difficult because we don't know – 'Why did this happen?', 'Why did that happen?', 'What came over me?' Silence allows to rise into our consciousness all those things which are lurking in our subconscious, memories particularly.

The point of this for prayer is that in order to know God we must know ourselves. It is in God that we have our existence, or as St Paul puts it, that 'we live and move and exist' (Acts 17:28). What we are reflects God. So, what we do not know about ourselves means that corresponding knowledge of God is withheld from us. If there is a great deal in us that is buried, not only is our knowledge of God the poorer, but also, the ministry of the presence and love of God to us in those buried memories or attitudes, cannot be openly received. When we are silent, however, it is more difficult to hide those buried areas which God wants to bring to our notice. As he brings them to our attention, then we can get to know him in that area of our lives that has previously been hidden. In Gerry Hughes' words:

> Memories are mighty important. There is a sense in which we *are* our memories and memories affect the way we are. So, in silence, we get more in touch with ourselves. Being more in touch with ourselves, we must be more in touch with God. St Augustine prayed: ' . . . that I may know you; that I may know myself'. [In Latin, *noverim te; noverim me.*]
>
> So the silence is not a sort of discipline, in the sense of, 'There is something we don't like so it will do us good to be quiet'. It is much more sensible than that! It gives us the chance to get in touch with what is really going on.

A time of silent retreat, for example, has again and again proved to be a time of revelation, a spiritual breakthrough for many people, as my wife, Molly, and I have personally experienced. It is to give God the space, away from both outer and inner activity, for him to show us our inner selves and to address us.

We live in a very busy and stressful culture. We have to run to stand still. There is pressure of work and pressure of family life; it all has us constantly thinking, 'What must I do next?' We are constantly 'doing'. Some churches make us very busy with responsibilities such as teaching children, mid-week home groups, visiting, drop-in centres, committees, etc. All (or most) of these activities are very worthwhile. But, so easily we can hide behind all this busyness and never meet God. It is often only when God strips away all that 'we must do next', that we have the space to have profound dealings with him. Busy Christians need to make space for silence, such as on quiet days or retreats or private walks in the country. Gerry continued,

> Because there is so much whizzing around on the treadmill, people are longing for some sort of silence. So, things like hill-walking and walking in general, I believe, are much more popular in this country than they were before.

The inner silence, to which the outer silence contributes, is about allowing God to be God in us and to be the source and mover of our prayers. Gerry put it like this.

> One of the greatest obstacles in prayer is that we make too much effort and we think too much. Consequently, in our effort, we are so busy trying to pray, that it is almost as though God doesn't get a chance. St Paul, however, says, 'Unless the Spirit within us cries "Abba Father", we cannot speak these words'. As the ancients said of prayer, 'God praying in us'. Therefore, the more still we can be, the better the chance that God will pray in us.

True prayer is not something that we do on our own. It is something that God does in us, by his Spirit. Our approach, then, must be to be still and try and let God pray in us, rather than feel that it is all up to us.

Advice on Coming into Silence

It is easy to speak of an inner silence in which God is praying in us; it is much harder to begin to experience it. Gerry's advice is:

> Don't force it. And, therefore, try and avoid those things in prayer which are going to pull you away from silence – like, trying to work things out and too much intellectual activity. The ancients said of prayer, 'Heart speaks to heart'. If it is heart speaking to heart, then the attitudes are simple.
>
> Don't try to leap at silence, because the more you try, the more distracting thoughts, memories and images will probably come to you. You will end up your devotions in a thoroughly bad temper, and bite the head off the next person you meet. So don't try too hard. But rather, listen: 'Where is God?' God is where you are. Therefore, listen. Particularly listen to your heart, by which I mean listen to the moods, the feelings, the anxieties, the fears, the hopes, the ambitions. Just listen to them and particularly to the frustrations. Whether we are conscious of it or not, God is in fact at work in all of us, drawing us out beyond ourselves. One of the reasons why we feel frustration is because, somewhere in us, we know we're called to something greater; therefore, we feel frustrated either with ourselves and our own pettiness, or the pettiness of others around us. So what I am saying is that we are trying to listen to God at work, beneath all those things.

It is important to have a great confidence that God will lead us into inner silence, albeit by gradual development. Gerry continued,

> The wonderful thing is to reach the point where you really can be still. I find in my own praying that it takes a very long time even to reach that point of

stillness, and you can't force it just by trying to be still. It's an interesting exercise to try to be still, not just physically still, but to be still in the mind – to drive out all thoughts, distractions, images, and ideas, etc. But it is the most effective way of inviting every interesting thought, memory, imagining, you've ever had to come tumbling back in! So, it's a curious thing, the more you try to empty it, the more it seems to fill up; and, therefore, we can't leap at stillness. The stillness that I am talking about is something which only God can give us. But there are certain ways in which we can dispose ourselves in prayer, which make it more likely that we reach an inner stillness, never complete, but relatively still.

So-called Distractions

Teachers on prayer, like Ignatius, have helped us to see that before we reach stillness we must go through a process of engagement with the things that are clamouring within us. As Gerry put it,

> It is as though we are a great mansion with many rooms, and the rooms are full of screaming children. There is one having a tantrum about this, another having a tantrum about that; there's another hammering at the door in another place, and, before guests come in, God can call the children of God to be quiet. Otherwise, we won't be able to meet The Guest. Therefore, we have got to come to terms with that which is causing the screaming.

People who are seeking to enter into silence get quite upset about what they call distractions. Gerry firmly insisted that these so-called distractions are the raw material on which God is working in us. They are, therefore, to be looked at, even prized, and not dismissed in frustration. He told the story of a man for whom he was leading an eight-day retreat, and whom he encouraged to pray with his imagination.

I suggested that he take that passage in Matthew where Jesus leaves home to go down to be baptised by John in the Jordan, and I suggested to him, 'Why not imagine you are with Jesus on that journey? Talk to Jesus about his hopes, his expectations, his fears, and his apprehensions, as you go on your way down towards Jerusalem, to the Jordan. And talk to him about your own hopes and fears and apprehensions, about your own going back to your work at the end of this retreat.' So when I went to see him, he was sitting bolt upright in his chair. And he said, 'I've tried the imagination and it doesn't work. I tried to imagine Jesus. I saw this figure, and he turned into a clown figure, and he began doing cartwheels and handsprings, and generally playing the fool. So I stopped.'

What appeared to be a distraction was in fact for this man very important, and I got him to look at it. Why was he so surprised at Jesus doing the hand-springs and the cartwheels? And, as he looked, he realised that his image of Jesus was so divine that it was utterly incongruous that Jesus should play the fool. He was an inhuman Jesus, an inhuman Christ, a 'supreme Spirit alone existing of himself, and infinite in all perfections'. The retreatant then realised that he was basing his life on this image, of a divine Christ, and consequently he couldn't allow himself the equivalent of handsprings, cartwheels, or playing the fool. Although in words he believed in the humanity of Christ, he'd never thought of Jesus as *really* human. So that distraction in fact was showing him something extraordinarily important about

72

himself. And had he just driven it away he would have lost that valuable message.

Whenever we are approaching silence something important may come to light through what seems to be a distraction, as Gerry emphasises.

> Distractions. I was going to say, 'Welcome them.' At least, acknowledge what are called distractions, remembering that there is nothing existing which is, in itself, a distraction, because God is in everything. Therefore, when in our prayers things occur to us – it might be memories, feuds that we're having, rows that we're having, parties we're going to, or whatever – let the thoughts come in; and, as it were, present them to God. Have a brief look at them, and see, 'Are they helping me to continue this relationship with God, this conversation with God, or are they drawing me away from prayer?' If they are drawing you away from prayer, however spiritual or theological or ecclesiastical they may be, drop them. If they are leading you to prayer, however profane, bizarre, or stupid they may appear, stay with them and use them. What we term distractions are sometimes the most important part of our prayer.

Gerry continued to emphasise that God cannot be met outside our existence. The thoughts which flood in must be looked at, because they may be central to what God is trying to do with us. They may be about good or bad relationships. The so-called distractions about relationships which we enjoy draw us towards God, as we thank God for them. On the other hand, if we become aware of relationships which are wrong, then Gerry's advice is that we show them to God, and, as we face our unease, and perhaps, our inability to forgive, we can then address the need to come to a point of complete forgiveness.

In order to help with quietening the 'screaming children' in our minds there are some well-tried steps given by Ignatius. Gerry listed these.

Step 1   Before you start praying, stand for a moment or two a little away from where you are going to pray and just bring to mind what you are about. The pause for reflection helps.

Step 2   Preparatory prayer. 'Grant that everything within me may be directed to your service and praise.'

Step 3   Consider what is going to be the focus of your prayer or meditation.

Step 4   Petition for prayer. Ask that God will meet you and pray in you as you meditate.

Step 5   Begin seeking to focus as you have decided. If you are trying an imaginative contemplation from a Gospel story then start by putting yourself into the scene. Who is present? What are they saying? What are they doing? The questions take their course as we become part of the scene in our imagination.

Objects as a Focus for Prayer

Many people who practise silent prayer find it helpful to use an object as a focus for prayer. This is usually visual, but could be something to touch, held in the hands. I asked Gerry what use he made of objects as a focus for silent prayer.

I find objects very helpful in prayer. It depends what sort of a mood you are in. Sometimes I light a candle – that's a very great help. Also, I have an African crucifix that someone gave me once, with an African on the cross. It's a beautiful crucifix. It's very moving because somehow it is Christ identifying himself

74

with every single human being, and particularly with Africa today, where there is such poverty and such oppression. We know Christ is there. God is sharing in it with us.

Silent meditation, with the suffering Christ as the focus, leads us into quiet adoration of the God who suffers with all who are oppressed. We realise that he is wounded, for example, with the Angolans, struggling with a war fought in their land, financed by outside powers in their interests and where many innocent children are being killed by land mines. We see also that Christ suffers with those who have to scrape a living in 'informal housing', on the edge of big cities like Johannesburg, and he suffers with those driven out from their homes for tribal reasons, and with all those in refugee settlements where disease and hunger are rife. All this is worship and praise of the God whose nature is to share our suffering.

Praise

At the heart of silent prayer is this appreciation of God himself. It does not need words, and Gerry's ideal is wordless prayer.

> If we could reach a certain stillness of mind and heart, and really be open, and really be still in prayer so that God could come to us, then I think prayer would be an 'Aah' of adoration. There would be no point in words if we could reach that point.

Nevertheless, we need not set words and silence in tension with each other, even if it is our words which so often smother silence. According to the Revelation of St John, silence plays a part in the worship of heaven (Revelation 8:1). But so do words. The living creatures cry out continually, 'Holy, holy, holy is the Lord God, the Almighty; he was, he is, and he is to come' (Revelation 4:8). So to use words is not an inferior way of praying. All our faculties are involved in relating to God. He made them all and is in them all.

Another dimension of silent praise is given by the sense of wonder in what we see around us, and especially what we admire in people. Gerry spoke of relishing those things and seeing how marvellous they are. He continued,

> The source of all true praise is appreciation, valuing, cherishing a person for what they've done and achieved, etc. So, similarly, we praise God when we praise his creation. That means always encouraging people to reflect on good memories when it comes to praying.

Listening

At the end of this chapter, the exercises focus around four areas of prayer: Praise, Listening, Intercession, Intimacy. If praise is not exactly fashionable in our society, listening certainly is. In our busy society many people long for someone to listen to them. Politicians or bishops, all stress that they will listen, though it is less clear that they do. Even banks claim to listen. Listening to God is spoken of in the Churches, again in a variety of styles. Everyone is emphasising listening.

Many Christians would say that they know what God has said to them. For some it is in the form of general awareness or direction. For others it is in a form of words, usually sensed, rather than heard audibly. But the scope for self-deception is obvious. I asked Gerry about his experience of God speaking to him.

> My first experience that I can remember of God was – I must have been about three, I suppose – sitting

on the edge of the bed, looking out of the window. I had been put to bed by my eldest sister. And I said, 'God'. I can still remember why I said, 'God' – to see what would happen when you said, 'God'. And nothing happened. So that was my first experience of addressing God and getting no answer. That's been the pattern ever since! I've never had an answer from God, certainly never a voice.

I can never say, 'Jesus said to me', or, 'God said to me', not in that way. On the other hand it is almost like a subtle sort of presence which doesn't speak words, but a kind of assurance, 'I am there'. So that when one reads in the Scripture, in the prophet Isaiah, 'Do not be afraid for I have redeemed you. I have called you by name. You are mine' (Isaiah 43:1), it makes sense. God doesn't need to speak. There are things to ask about and we can get clear answers. But God only speaks in a metaphorical sense. Yet, in the words of the prophets, the Lord says, 'Do not be afraid for I am with you.' It makes sense. Those words speak to something in experience.

The sense of God speaking is, for Gerry, not in words. Rather, it is a moment of realisation, or what he calls 'a curious sort of – being attracted by God, an inner longing'.

I'm obviously in the hand of some power far greater than I. And, beginning to realise our own individual tininess and utter fragility, we're caught up in something much greater. I look at the picture, the portrait of Jesus, as the Gospels present him, and see this most attractive human being, who takes a piece of bread and breaks it, and says to his friends, 'This is me given for you. Do this in my memory.' We are told by St Paul that this Jesus is the image of the unseen God. So this is telling me what God is like,

77

the nature of the God who holds all things in union. Therefore, the whole of reality around us is transformed into that reality, the living God around us.

A Christ who took a body, and lived as a human, is a Christ who is at home in matter. In him, the 'Word', God, holds everything together. Every Eucharist or service of Holy Communion is a sign of this.

Gerry stresses that God's communication with us has to come through all the raw material of our lives. He finds that it takes the form of these moments of realisation, about ourselves and about God.

> I'm always chary about people saying, 'The Lord has said to me'. He always seems to speak so like the characters he has 'spoken' to, and shares the same prejudices! But I think if we have ears, if we have the perception, everything speaks, and can speak of God to us.

Since knowing God and knowing ourselves are so bound up together, listening in silence is about listening to ourselves, so as to know what is going on inside. Gerry sees this is the way we can come to be aware of the love of God.

> We must listen to the restlessness and the emptiness, the distress and the longing of our own heart. That's where God is. We look on all those things as negatives. They can also be a joy, and wonderful. As we listen to the distress, so God will lead us beyond it. But first we must be aware of it, through experience. People who, through upbringing, have experienced a lack of love, who have had a tough time, and whose resolve is not strong, given a little encouragement, the love can come to life again. But it needs the company of people who will set the person on their feet.

To practise the art of being still, then, in order to

listen, is to provide a rich playground for real relationships with God to grow. We can discover who we are and what he is. As we listen to our moods and feelings, our anxieties, ambitions and frustrations, Gerry's advice is that we present them back to God, asking him to show us what it all means and where the thoughts are leading. The reason for our frustrations may be that we have expectations that are totally awry, and by holding to them we are stifling ourselves. Listening enables God to interpret our experience for us. It gives space for change and our attitudes can be altered.

Intercession

When our conversation moved to the subject of intercessory prayer, prayer for others, through silence, we were quickly on to the problem of lists. Lists can become a tyranny, Gerry argued. Those of us who have used them for years know that this is true. Gerry commends the same relaxed approach to intercession as to listening, following the promptings of God rather than the discipline of working with lists of people to pray for.

> I've never really seen the point of prayer lists because I think, 'God knows all this'. What I like to do, mainly for my own sake, is to decide, 'I'm going to remember X or Y.' But it's very quick.
>
> If I had a list of people to get through and pray for, that for me would not be silent prayer. On the other hand, what I have found helpful, particularly when I was on long walks, was to decide to pray for others, and instead of having a little list, just walking along and seeing who pops up. Then, as it were, I see them and hand them over to God who knows what to do about him or her. But that is very different from working through a list.

The problem with lists is that control is kept in our own

hands, so we can be diverted from allowing God to be God, and do his praying within us. The complementary truth, however, is that God has called us to relate to him as children to a father, and children ask their parents, in a natural way, about that for which they are concerned. Children, however, also learn to share in the particular concerns of their parents. This brings us back to God as the author of prayer. God is concerned for all people and we learn to share that concern with him. Or as Jesus taught us to pray to God the Father in the Lord's Prayer, 'Your Kingdom come; your will be done'. Lists may help us to share that concern intelligently, whether our intercession is silently holding people before God or praying in words, silently or out loud. However we use our silent prayer for intercession, we must remember that God is the author of true prayer, and we are not to behave as if it all depends on us. Gerry again spoke helpfully,

I think with intercession it becomes a kind of tyranny, almost, for some people. It becomes a misery because they can't remember all the people they've got to pray for. It is almost as though there is no God, or God is totally absent-minded, and if he is not reminded by me then he is going to take it out on them! Whereas I think of prayers of intercession as, see what turns up, and make sure of commending people to God, obviously family and friends, but also enemies. That's important, to pray for our enemies.

Intimacy

In the last of the four exercises in the course material at the end of this chapter, we are invited, in silence, to explore the love of God and our response to it, possibly with a candle as a focal point. Gerry thinks that a candle somehow serves to evoke a sense of the bond between us and God. He explained why he thought that candles were so helpful in silent prayer.

It's full of symbolism: Christ, the Light of the world. But I think it touches something in us. This is why, universally, people are fascinated by candlelight, particularly candles in the dark. The candlelight dispels the darkness; it does it gently, it gives warmth. And somehow that is speaking to something inside us, the longing to dispel the darkness within, and to be a giver of warmth. Perhaps it is the desire that one's life should be transformed into light, as the candle is into the candle flame.

Gerry had a final reminder on the subject of intimacy. We must not delude ourselves or put on an act. We are capable in prayer of turning even times of silent prayer into times when we indulge ourselves or deceive ourselves, just as we can do with spoken prayer. God wants to meet us as we are, and true prayer must proceed from complete honesty with ourselves.

Just be rigorously honest, or try to be, without any pretence. It is very difficult to be honest. Not even pretending that I like this prayer when I am bored out of my mind. God is in truth. I can't think of a better way, any other way of intimacy with God, other than totally, as far as you can, be honest.

Silent prayer spreads before us a rich tapestry woven by God. Important and natural though words are, just to pray pouring out endless words is to put obstacles in the way of truly meeting God, and letting him pray in us and change us. Learning silent prayer lets God in.

GROUP STUDY

In pairs, or as a group, say something about how your prayer has been during the past week. Share any questions or difficulties, as well as what has been good, new and enriching.

As a group, sit in silence for about three minutes, listening to and noticing all the different sounds that you can hear. At the end of the three minutes, tell each other what you heard.

Sit in silence for another three minutes. This time, 'listen' to all that is going on inside you: your thoughts, feelings, tension, etc. Share as much as you want about how you found that experience.

Different kinds of silence

There are many different situations and experiences in life that cause us to be silent. Below are just some of the kinds of silence that we encounter in everyday living.

waiting	intimacy	watching
listening	sleeping	shock
thinking	grief	amazement
hostility	uncertainty	in the bath!

 Share some examples of silences that you have enjoyed or valued. Then share some examples of silence that you have found uncomfortable. Think about what it was that caused that discomfort. If it was embarrassment, what were you embarrassed about? If you were afraid, what were you afraid of?

In the group, talk about the different things that we do to avoid silence, both when we are alone and when we are with other people.

Silence can be comfortable or uncomfortable. What sorts of things make the difference between comfortable and uncomfortable silence?

Something to read

You may have found in your discussion so far, that you have rather mixed feelings about silence. Sometimes you long for it, sometimes you avoid it.

This mixture of feelings is something that we also experience about other things that are important to us; e.g. love, intimacy, friendship, independence, truth, and even God.

We know these things are important for our well-being and we want them. Our instincts and desires lead us towards them. Yet, because we are broken and vulnerable, we are afraid of being seen as we really are, of being rejected or hurt. So we want to draw back.

As we think of exploring prayer through silence, we are not considering a silence that is totally empty. It is not a silence which leaves us alone, without God. It is a silence in which he is very much with us, as he has promised, 'I will never leave you or forsake you' (Hebrews 13:5).

It is important to remember how much God loves us, and that he wants only the very best for us.

Just as there can be many kinds of silence in the company of other people, so there can be with God. Silence with him can be praise, delight, adoration, intercession, listening, reaching out, self offering, simply being together, and much more.

Silent prayer is part of our communication with God. Sometimes it seems as if it is we who decide what our prayer is to be about. Silence in prayer involves opening ourselves to God, to his initiative, and being willing to listen to him.

⁂

If you are using the cassette tape, listen now to the interview with Gerard W. Hughes.

In pairs, discuss what forms of silent prayer you have found helpful or unhelpful. If you wish and as much as you wish, share any occasions when memories have surfaced during silence which have led you to personal growth or healing.

Here are four 'tasters' of prayer through silence. Try as many as you can in the time available. Each one should last for about five minutes and should be led by the group leader. You may like to use different bodily postures (standing, sitting or kneeling), and you need not all use the same one.

Praise

Choose one aspect of God's character that you *really* appreciate: something about God that makes you proud of him, or pleased to know him.

You may like to visualise God, or Jesus, and try to 'see' that quality in him. Alternatively, hold the words, 'God is (*that quality*)' in your mind.

Think what you could do with your hands or body to help you in this prayer of praise.

Delight in God and wonder at this quality in him. Hold this attitude of silent praise until the leader brings it to an end with a prayer or song of praise.

Listening

If you have an issue that concerns you, or an important question to ask God, bring that silently to him. Then wait for his answer.

If you have no particular issue or question, then pray silently, 'Lord, what do you want to say to me?' and wait for his answer.

Keep waiting and 'listening' to God. If something that seems as if it might be an answer comes to you (it may be a hunch, a picture, a feeling, words, or something else), stay with it, holding it before God, offering it to him to adjust or change. Trust God to use the silence you have offered him.

Remain waiting and listening until the leader brings the time to a close.

Intercession

Choose a person or situation for which you wish to pray and hold them up to God. You may find it helpful to lift up your hands and imagine yourself lifting this person, or situation, towards God.

We naturally tend to start our prayer by focusing on the problem; you may find that it helps your faith more to start by concentrating on God. Focus on his goodness, his gentleness or whatever aspect of God is appropriate to your prayer. Then bring your need for prayer into the picture.

Continue to hold this need before God.

Intimacy

In whatever way you find best, know and be aware that God is close to you. You may wish to focus on God as Father, as Jesus, or as Holy Spirit. Sense that he loves you and is showing his love to you.

People choose to imagine God in different ways: looking at them lovingly; as Jesus on the cross; some find it easier to imagine God behind them or beside them. You could use a picture or icon.

Respond to this by letting your love flow out to God. Allow yourself to enjoy simply being with him.

After each exercise, or after all those that you have time for, share together what you found helpful or unhelpful.

If there are any thoughts arising from the corresponding sections of this chapter, discuss them too.

Closing prayer

In a moment of silence, each hold up to God the person on your right and then the person on your left. Finish the meeting by saying the Grace together.

DURING THE WEEK

- Repeat the prayer exercises from this session, especially those that you found most helpful. If you did not have time for all of them, try any that you missed.
- Try to give at least five minutes to silent prayer each day. Experiment to find which ways into stillness suit you best at present (this may change with time). It can be hard to find silence, not simply shutting out physical sounds, but also quietening the inner 'noise' of our own thoughts and busyness. We need to be still inwardly as well as outwardly. Some of the following suggestions may help:

  Ask God to quieten you.

  Relax: Tense your muscles and then relax them. Do this with all the different parts of your body in turn.

  Breathe normally, gently and regularly. Be aware of your breathing, in and out.

  A word or phrase, steadily repeated: e.g. 'Lord, have mercy on me'; 'Jesus'; 'I love you, Lord'; 'Peace'; 'Come, Holy Spirit'.

  An object to look at: e.g. a flower, cross, picture, stone or candle.

  A mental picture: e.g. Jesus, the Father, the cross, a peaceful scene of land, sea or sky, a favourite place.

  Music: a tape (song or instrumental); sing a verse of a hymn or song (Taizé chants can be helpful).

  A verse of Scripture, repeated or written out to look at: e.g. **Psalm 46:10**; **Matthew 11:28**; **John 14:27**.

- You may find that distractions crowd into your mind, making stillness and inner silence difficult. If so, you may find that it helps to lift the distracting thoughts to God, to jot them down on a piece of paper for later or perhaps simply to ignore them and let them go away.
- Read chapter 5 of this book, 'Praying through Life'.

Session 5

Praying through Life

with Angela Tilby

We have looked at prayer through words, through Scripture and through silence, and all our 'guides' have shown that each pathway of prayer is interwoven with the others and indeed with the whole of life. We relate to God through all that we are.

Everything in life is to be viewed in the awareness of where we truly belong, at 'home' in God. At the human level 'home' is always in the back of our minds, whether we are actually there or not. It is a place of permanence, not a place we visit occasionally. In a similar way, our aim is to learn to know where we belong, spiritually, and to live in constant relationship with our spiritual home, whether we are praying or not. Home is in God; so prayer and life are welded together as one.

Angela Tilby is a well-known broadcaster and TV producer, as well as being a theologian and author. When we met in my home in London I began by asking her what events in her daily life made her most aware of God.

I used to feel that you had to be aware of God as you went about your daily life, all the time, that one was looking for a kind of constant consciousness and awareness. I've come to realise that it doesn't quite work like that, that praying is about doing what you are doing wholeheartedly; and you are aware of God, not always at the time, but in reflection afterwards. So, if I think, 'When are the moments in the day when I am aware of God?', it's at those moments, I think, when I feel connected, or I feel understanding, or I feel linked to what is going on around me, or simply in touch with it, with the feelings of it.

Now, at the time of having those feelings, God may not be on my mind. It's in the reflection afterwards that I realise – that's where God was, and, therefore, that's where God is.

We know that God is always there and close. He doesn't move his presence towards and away from us, according to how much we are aware of him. Rather, we are trying to grow in the sense that we are always 'at home', although we cannot always be thinking about him.

We decorate our homes according to individual taste. We choose and place the furniture and the pictures because that particular arrangement does something for us. It is the home we look forward to coming home to. In a similar way, in seeking to find this underlying awareness of our lives in God, the moments of life which brim over with vitality are important. They may be about the surroundings of our lives. They may be about the relationships. They are one way in which our awareness of God grows, for he is the giver of all life and energy. Times which stir us with vitality and energy are glimpses of God's true presence.

I asked Angela to elaborate on the occasions which released in her the energy which she had learnt to see as a sign of God. For her, it was those moments in her work which spelt out something of the nature of God's creation.

> I am speaking as somebody who works in media, who works in words, who works in images. It's when, if I am making a television programme, you suddenly see how a particular sequence of images can convey an emotion. It's when you see how photography can quite suddenly set things alongside each other and bring them to life. It's an artistic, creative area for me, when suddenly the 'word' comes forth and you don't know where it has come from, but there it is.

The current Christian images of God have not been strong on the truth that God is in all creation. We think of him as transcendent, as 'other' than us and the world, as its creator. We think of him as the loving Father, and as personal, seen in the nature of Jesus Christ. Yet, it is equally true that the vibrant energy of every atom is God's energy. There is no other ultimate source of energy. God is *in everything*, and the created universe is a sign or sacrament of him.

In speaking of moments when God is recognised, Angela likens this capacity in the life of people to priestliness, because it is presenting a sacrament, that is, a sign of God.

> You could be baking a cake. You could be driving a car. Whatever it is, in that moment of beauty, when you recognise that you are bringing something forth, you are articulating something which is already there, but it is coming through you in a fresh way. That's a moment of recognition of God. It's a very specifically human moment; and, I say, priestly, because I think that's what it's really about.

Something of the character of the artist is always revealed in the work of art. God has revealed himself in the way life is. There are moments when this awareness breaks through. I asked Angela to put in simple words just what it is that she then declares as 'This is God'.

> If one is thinking of someone who is working with their hands, it's often just doing it, with mindfulness. You are aware of the dough in your hands. You are aware of the shaping. You are aware, in a way, of the lovely fact that cold hands can make good pastry. It's as simple as that. And, in a sense, the givenness of that is something that will give you a flow of energy. You will feel good about it. You will know that you are competent and that you can do it, that you have got the co-ordination between hand and brain and measuring and ingredients, and all the rest of it. And

the satisfaction and energy that comes of that is a moment of grace. It's a moment when you know you are a creature and you can just say, 'Help', 'Thank you', 'Here I am'. Those are the basic ingredients of prayer for all of us.

Finding God in the Desolation

There is another side to this which is about those times when we are stripped of what we love to do and do naturally, and of the relationships which belonged to that activity. Angela put it like this,

> It's particularly hard, I think, when people have to change what they're doing. Illness, or age, or whatever, takes you out of the thing you've been doing naturally, and you have to learn how to be a priestly human being in a different sort of way. Suddenly all the relationships are withdrawn and you're on your own. How do I then find God in this diminished state, as it seems? How do I find God when I'm not able to do the things I could do once? I've had periods of illness, not enormously serious, but temporarily disabling, when it's felt as if all the sunshine has gone out. One is struggling to make sense of emptiness and disability for periods of time. And you can't at the time. It's afterwards that you see that a dark side of God, a sort of grace of quiet, and actionless, and void, was also a new face of the Almighty that one was being given at that moment.

So there is another face of God, so to speak, which we can only learn through what is not giving us positive experiences. We have to allow ourselves just to receive, or to be 'done to'. The Gospels tell us how, at a certain point in the Passion story, Jesus allowed himself to be 'handed over' for the crucifiers to do their worst. But it was all in the plan of God. And, as W. H. Vanstone has shown in his well-known book, *The Stature of Waiting*, Jesus has given dignity to all those times when we cannot be in control, but have to receive whatever comes to us. Then we discover that God accomplishes his plan. Or as Angela put it, speaking of the time when her own father was unable to be active any more,

> I have a feeling that unless we've been there, we don't know much about grace. If we are always doing to others and for others, when are we receiving from the servant, the servant God?

It is common Christian testimony that it is the times when life is hard, and when God may seem to be absent, that are times of great personal and spiritual growth. God uses such times to wean us away from our own achievements and successes to depend upon him, and to love him for who he is, regardless of the circumstances of our lives, positive or negative.

Angela shared with me another interesting experience of desolation. It was about her reaction to public tragedy, and how she found that a sense of 'blocking' had inhibited her praying. It was as if she felt ashamed that this was the way things are in God's world.

> I've been rather aware of something which comes over me if there's a very public tragedy, or even a private one. I feel a reluctance to pray. I feel that it's quite difficult to. I think it's a kind of anger and a feeling of, 'If this can happen, I don't know that I want to spend time acknowledging it, getting close to a God who is around in a world where this kind of thing can happen'.
>
> I remember some years ago, when the Challenger disaster happened, and that was so awful. There was something so shaming about humanity in that. This wonderful device went off like a firework, and then,

you watched on television, and it fell back to earth; and one suddenly was aware that those people were being very publicly killed. It was a most awful moment. And I think I did feel sort of ashamed to be in the presence of God at that point, because it seemed the universe was just such a mess. I think you would then have to be very brave about approaching God, in a way, and work against one's instincts to shut down, to hide and to feel shame and failure too acutely.

We went on to speak of the tragic events of Dunblane in March 1996, when a gunman broke into a school and shot a teacher and pupils. I asked Angela if she found the same block to her prayers.

Very much so, yes. I felt very tearful about that and hugely shocked and shaken. I did find it hard to pray. Was it anger? Was I angry with God that it had happened? It's more like a sort of shame, as if the whole experience exposed us to something about our human nature that we just can't deal with. So you almost go back to God as a sinner, and that's a hard thing to do, isn't it?

Something within me responds to what Angela is saying. I remember similar feelings in me when the *Herald of Free Enterprise* sank, and also at the start of the Gulf War. Molly and I were sitting up in bed, just before midnight, watching the first news flashes as the shelling began. I remember the most dreadful leaden feeling in my stomach as war started, and wondering how human beings managed to live in such an appalling way in God's world.

A few weeks later I arrived in Berlin as part of a sabbatical, still very aware of the ongoing Gulf War. I entered the tower, which is still standing, of the Kaiser Wilhelm Gedächtniskirk (Kaiser Wilhelm Memorial

Church). All the rest of the church had been destroyed in the Second World War. After looking briefly at the pictures of the destruction of the church and city, I had to go out quickly into the new church, kneel down, and sob with anguish for half an hour.

Finding God in Daily Reflection

In the safety and security of our homes we are fed, physically and emotionally. There is the security to make mistakes, to laugh and to grow as people. The review of the day, with God, is like that. What were the positive experiences? What were the negative points? If I wish to learn how to respond better to the love of God tomorrow, I must review my response today. I asked Angela how she reflected on the day's events.

I have to confess I'm not good at this. I am a morning person. I get up early in the morning and God is much more around for me at 6 or 7 a.m. in quiet and with the Scriptures and the Psalms. I usually say a form of daily office and my great temptation is then to forget it until the next day. But I know that Ignatius is such an important teacher of Christian prayer. He would say, 'If everything else goes, your reflection at the end of the day must not. Forget saying the office; forget your morning Psalms; the really important bit is reflecting back.' So I try to take that on board, and do it, but I don't do it for as long as I'd like.

Having said that, what is it about? I think it's about tracing the kind of energy flows that have happened in the day. I don't tend to go back minutely over every event. What I try to do is to ask, 'Can I think of three occasions today when I've really had that sense of flow of energy, that it's been going out in a positive whole, in a together sort of way? Can I mark up those three moments?' And then, from a reflection on that, 'What was it that made me think that way?'

I think you are then in a position to face three moments when the opposite happened and when there was a sense of frustration, of disintegration that you weren't whole, that you were being torn apart in some way or another. And then I leave these six 'dips' in the hands of God.

Not everyone will do this on a daily basis, but the process of reflection on our daily experience must be there. The point is that we must build up a reflective approach to our lives so that the pattern of conversion can steadily continue. God is drawing us to himself all the time, teaching us to respond to his love.

Here is an outline for this process of reflection. It can be used with the outline for group or personal study at the end of this chapter. Some call it the Examen, or Prayer of Awareness.

Step 1 Thank God for particular elements in the day.

Step 2 Ask the Holy Spirit to open your eyes to see the meaning of the day from God's perspective and to reveal what he wants us to notice.

Step 3 Play back the day, thinking through where we have been, whom we have met, what we have done. We notice what it has been like without judging ourselves.

Step 4 Notice:
– times we were drawn to God.
– times we were driven by expectations, our own, or those of others.
– times when right or good things happened.
– times of disturbance, pain or unease.

Step 5 Allow ourselves to become conscious of sin we have committed. We say we are sorry and ask for forgiveness.

Step 6 Turn to the Lord in our helplessness. Talk things over with him, telling him our true feelings and sensing his compassion, his understanding, and his love for us however we are feeling. If we learn to trust God, then we can come to a deeper acceptance of our weakness.

The importance of confession (Step 5) is worth emphasising. It is the way God puts right what is wrong in his world. He forgives us completely. It is over as far as God is concerned. Then we need his help if there is a need to restore any human relationships which have been broken.

We live in a generation which is reluctant to speak of sin. It is a society which both looks for someone to blame for everything, and is highly defensive. This is a pity. God's way is that we firmly own our wrongdoing, without minimising it, and he then deals with it completely, by forgiving it. We can own our fault, because it is then forgiven.

Angela grew up in a Christian tradition which provided a check-list of sins so that confession could be made thoroughly.

You were supposed to go through the list every time you went to Holy Communion and tick off: 'Have I been horrid to my parents? Have I kept the Ten Commandments? Have I done this or that thing?' I always found that a most desolating experience because the check-list approach never seemed to really get inside one's awareness and consciousness. I'm sure it has its virtues, and for some people it would be a jolly good way of doing a kind of self-examination. But it just seemed to leave me feeling that I had done everything wrong, and even if I hadn't, then I was just being proud. Either way round it didn't work. But I do find the sense of just trying to dip in and out of my day, finding the moments when the energy flow was positive, and when it wasn't, and why, very, very useful.

When we become aware of sin there is also a place for thanksgiving as I well remember in my own teenage years. To feel God putting his finger on what was wrong, in order that I might change, was also the assurance that God had not given up on me. Somehow, I knew that he was only doing it to make the best of me.

Returning to Ignatius, and the purpose of the daily prayer of awareness, Angela said,

> The thing I think that Ignatius wants you to take from it, is not a sort of judgement on yourself: 'I did this bit badly, and this bit right'. But just beginning to observe what are the kind of things that bring you together, bring you to wholeness and peace; and what are the kind of things that do the opposite. That then works back into your daily experience. It's just a nudging, a fine tuning, if you like, of how you are in the world and how well you know yourself. That's really what the Examen [the prayer of awareness] is about; and over time it works.

Returning to Step 6, this is about telling the Lord our true feelings, but not only the Lord. Angela believes that coming to true self-knowledge is about accepting ourselves within the context of wider relationships. She put it like this.

> I have always felt a bit of a struggle within Christian culture. We are encouraged to be rather self-sufficient and to cultivate an image that is untroubled, unangry, that doesn't hate, that doesn't ever despair. And if we do hate or are angry or despair, we do it very privately and don't let it be known or seen. I think there is something not terribly healthy about living in that sort of armour, and we've all been

encouraged to do it, I think. It's partly a sort of English thing. But it's a sort of Christian thing as well. And I feel that breakthroughs have come for me when I am able to know myself as a very angry, hateful and fragmented being, and to know that that self is accepted by God, as it is. I don't have to be good to pray. It's very difficult, because everything in one's psyche encourages you to think, 'I must be whole before I can approach God'. Of course, it's absolutely not true. We must be broken.

Praying at all Times

The words of St Paul, 'Pray constantly' (I Thessalonians 4:17), seem somewhat daunting and even unreasonable! That is, until we see that this is about learning to live in constant awareness of where we truly belong. Home is always with us, whether we are consciously thinking about it or not. Praying at all times is best understood as a similar constant relationship with where we belong, that is, in God.

In any home, conversation has a natural place, indeed, words lie very much at the heart of the relationships there. But being at home and belonging to those who are there, is so much more than the words spoken. So it is with praying at all times. Speech to God is natural, and it is good to address him all through the day. Some people speak of 'arrow prayers', those quick prayers that we shoot off to God all through the day. They should be real, and about our feelings and our needs, or for others and their needs, or for God's great concerns. They can be full of thanksgiving, or simple words to say 'sorry'. As we journey, our 'arrow' prayers will reflect more closely the heart of God and the passion he has for his will to be done in all the world.

In a happy home, those who speak must listen. As we

saw in the last chapter, it is important to be giving space so as to be aware of what God is showing us or saying to us. In a home, however, there is all the warmth and security that comes from being in the same house, whether we are thinking about it or not. And when we are away from home, all the security that our place of belonging provides is with us, though mostly unconsciously. So, 'Pray constantly' begins to look like, 'Learn to know where you belong, and live in constant relationship with your spiritual home'.

When I asked Angela how she would help somebody to understand how to pray at all times, she replied,

> I love that story of the commander at the battle of Marston Moor who said to God, 'I am going to be very busy today. I won't be able to remember you, but please remember me.' I think that is what praying at all times is. You can't be conscious of God the whole time and actually you shouldn't be. If the surgeon doing the operation is thinking about God whilst he is wielding the scalpel he won't be doing the job properly. I think that it is about finding the moments where you sum up the dedication, but then you get on with it.

Then Angela asked me if I prayed all day. I replied that I didn't, and was comfortable with not doing so, although I wished I did so more than I do. It seems to me that just as awareness of home is with us during the day, even when we are not thinking about it, so it is possible to grow into a way of living in which there is a not fully conscious, but real, awareness of God as the events of the day unfold. The 'arrow prayers' mentioned above then tend to flow naturally, and not just when in straits of desperation!

Homes differ, and in some homes there will be many fewer words spoken than in others. But the sense of belonging is no less. Angela spoke, movingly, about people whose awareness of God is largely without words. Aware of his presence in creation as they shape the dough or make the pastry, they would find it hard to start saying words like 'Thank you, God'.

Some people can't say it in those words because they have a difficulty with intimacy with God. It's sometimes a feeling about a personal unworthiness and also partly a feeling that God is so big that to speak to God is somehow to diminish him. I sometimes feel that there are people like that who are almost natural contemplatives. They are beyond words; they are not people who can find the thing to say, but in their commitment and devotion – the wordless sense of wonder. They are praying, but in a different key. I've met farmers and bakers and those in launderettes who pray in a very unverbal way, and would feel affronted by words, in some way. The God they are in touch with is so close that a word gets in the way.

Daily Awareness Needs Daily Rhythm

The aim, then, is to learn to live 'at home' with God. What will help us to develop this rhythm in life? Clearly, if prayer is simply an occasional choice, 'I think I'll pray tonight', rather as one might decide to go to the pub, or visit a restaurant, the rhythm will not be created. Prayer is not something that should be competing with all our other interests for a space. To develop a constant sense of living with God, the rhythm needs to be developed on a daily basis. Specific time must be set aside for God each day, so that the rhythmic attitude, 'my life is in God and for God', is built up. The same is true, in my judgement, for acts of daily worship in schools.

I asked Angela what straightforward advice she

would give to somebody who was wanting to be prayerful in all they do.

> One hates saying this, but it is actually true: you have got to set aside some time. For most people it may not be daily at first, but it will become so. I don't think one should push oneself ridiculously, but you've got to actually safeguard time. Now, I don't think it matters when that is. I am a morning person. I'd hate to have a regular evening time for prayer; it would really wind me up. But you have to know yourself which is your best time; and people are more or less flexible. For some people it would need to be exactly the same time every day. Others would know that as long as they did it between this sort of hour and that, it would be OK. But I don't feel you can get out of that one. You can't pray unless you actually do it.

I would agree with that. I have always been grateful that at the time of my personal commitment to Christ, when I was twelve years old, I was taught to spend time each day in reading the Bible and in prayer. I started this daily pattern at bedtime. Frequently, I fell asleep on my knees and my mother would come in and put me into bed.

As to the content of prayer, I started with simple requests and thanksgivings. Like Angela, I began with daily Bible reading notes and read the passage set for the day. Then I prayed. Both of us learnt a well-known framework, ACTS: Adoration; Confession; Thanksgiving; Supplication.

Usually, however, I preferred my prayers to be more spontaneous. Sometimes I would be particularly penitent. Other times there would be much thanksgiving. I have used lists of those I wish to pray for, and still do. As the years have unfolded, I have sung hymns or songs, played Taizé tapes, and sat quietly in the Lord's arms, too tired to make many requests. I have worked hard at praise or thanksgiving, prayed as I walked, early in the mornings, enjoyed silence, focused on a candle, crucifix or icon, or prostrated myself. I have made requests silently and out loud, sometimes very vigorously. I have shared excruciating pain with God and done little more than just stay with him when everything else I prized seemed to be stripped away. What a journey it is! But as one who has been at it for over forty years, my testimony is that it is an adventure which brings a rich harvest of joy and peace. Angela said the same.

We live in the age of a quick fix. But prayer does not change you just like that. It's the years of it. It's rather like dieting, in a way. You know, it's all very well losing your two stone, but only if you keep the regular pattern going does it become part of your life. You are going to go like a yoyo, a spiritual yoyo. I was for years. It took me about ten or twelve years for prayer to become established in any real way. I would do it for a bit and then stop. But, eventually, the lovely thing about it all is that, if Ignatius is right, there is a sort of magnetic compass mark in the soul that does, in the end, if you give it enough time and space, orientate itself towards its true North. And it's magnetic; you are drawn by the love of God, in the end.

Sadly, many people get stuck because they lack the courage to try other things. They feel guilty for not doing what they think they ought to be doing, instead of trying something different. Maybe they don't listen enough to a range of ideas from other people and say, 'I'll try that'. It's such a pity when different kinds of recipes might just lead to something much more satisfying. As Angela said,

You have got to begin somewhere and I think you

103

will only find, as you do it, what works for you and what doesn't. It was ages afterwards that I began to realise that meditating on the single line of part of a psalm could actually hold me, and bring me to an experience of God of a quite different quality. But I had to discover that and then trust that that was all right, that you could sometimes abandon the ACTS in order to do something else. It is trial and error, I'm afraid! I think you've got to give yourself the freedom to experiment a bit. Usually the sense that a way of prayer is dying is very obvious and the pain that it causes to try and go on in the way that has died prods you into finding something else.

I hope these five sessions have encouraged you to pray. Prayer yields such rich rewards. But it has to be worked at; and everyone's journey is different, personal to you and God, but in company with thousands of others. May God bless you as you continue your pathway to home.

GROUP STUDY

Quieten yourself and become still in your inner being. Remind yourself of the loving presence of God there, where you are your real self with no masks. Speak to the Lord simply about how you are feeling now – perhaps at the end of a busy day – and what it is like for you to be here. Share in the group something about how the week has been for you.

In the centre of all our chaotic experience God is there, ceaselessly inviting us to a deeper awareness of his presence with us and for us; drawing us to himself through Jesus Christ. Read **John 6:37 and 44**.

Spend a few minutes in silence. Ask yourself: what kind of things lead me to God? In what ways do I find I am drawn to the Lord? Where and when do I feel closest to God? What activities and situations bring me to life and send me outwards?

Share something of what you have discovered. You need only say as much as you feel comfortable with.

St Ignatius of Loyola

St Ignatius of Loyola (sixteenth century) was a rather nominal Christian in his early life and something of a romantic. He became a soldier, was wounded in battle and had to spend a long time in convalescence in the castle belonging to his brother at Loyola.

He asked for books to pass the time but the only ones available were romantic tales of chivalry and lives of the saints. He read both, avidly.

When reading the former he felt elated and excited. He dreamt of winning the hand of a beautiful lady by noble deeds. When reading the lives of the saints he also felt excited. He admired their bravery and courage.

After some time an important discovery dawned on him. While reading both types of writing he felt alive and stimulated, but afterwards there was a difference.

After reading the romances he felt listless and dejected; after reading the lives of the saints he continued to feel full of enthusiasm and an overwhelming desire to imitate them.

One was leaving him drawn to the Lord and his service; the other made him feel driven to a sense of futility and therefore away from God. This was the beginning of an ever-deepening process of discernment in the life of Ignatius.

There are many events, things or people which make us aware of God make us feel alive or aware of the rightness of what we are doing. Things that arouse our desire to live for God, or make us realise that our life is important to him.

On the other hand, we can feel flat, bored, dissatisfied, unhappy, disjointed or low in spirit. Then we do not seem to experience God. He seems far away. Sometimes these moods and feelings are strong, sometimes more subtle. We often ignore them, hardly notice them, or simply grit our teeth and carry on.

 In silence, reflect for a while and ask yourself: what activities, situations and things drag me down, keep me enclosed in myself and make God seem far away?

 In pairs, share something of what you have discovered. You need only say what you feel comfortable about.

 In the chapter, Angela Tilby describes various things which make her aware of God (pp. 89–92). In the group, discuss the things that make you aware of God.

If you are using the cassette tape, listen to the interview with Angela Tilby.

 Share how you have reacted to news of public tragedy and how, in the light of the disaster, your prayer has been affected.

Praying at all times
St Paul writes about 'praying at all times'. Of course we cannot be consciously praying all the time, in the sense

of concentrating on God, but we can learn to be aware always that he is with us.

We seek to move through life with God and let God move with us. It is being with God that changes us **(2 Corinthians 3:18 and Acts 4:13)**. This is to do with our inner disposition, a growing, habitual way of living. We are trying to become more and more identified with Christ, so that we think and act and speak out of that inner reality.

 In the group, share any things that stood out for you, about praying at all times, from either this chapter or the tape. Here are some of the interpretations mentioned:

> Being aware that God is with us
> Remembering that God always remembers us
> Finding the moments when we sum up our
>   dedication to God
> Learning to know where we belong
> Living in constant relationship with our spiritual
>   home
> Sharing our experience of the day with God as we
>   go along

Discuss your own understanding of the call to 'pray at all times'.

Consider together how important it is to build a daily routine of prayer. Share your own experience of such a routine.

Prayer of awareness

Something to read

We are often blown about by our inward feelings and moods. But if we can learn to notice them and 'read' them, if we can be more reflective, then we will begin to

107

realise where God is and become more and more aware of what leads us away from him, as well as what draws us to him.

Deep in the Christian tradition is this practice of reflective prayer or 'prayer of awareness'. It is a regular reflection on our experience.

If we live unreflective lives we miss so much of life's meaning. To give a little time, perhaps at the end of a day, to this 'looking back to be aware', will awaken us to God's presence and activity in the whole of our experience, not just in our prayer times.

Giving time for reflection also leads us to a greater desire for prayer. We begin to realise that in our deepest feelings the Father is drawing us to himself. At the same time we realise that our sinful nature (all that still needs healing in us) can easily take us away from him.

In doing this, we will find positive things, such as a joy when we make the effort to pray, or do what we think God wants.

We will also find negative things, for example, that we get moody and irritable or need a lot of affirmation from others. This can also be positive, if we rejoice in this new self-awareness and thank God for it. We can then ask him to forgive us, heal us and help us to respond differently.

If we expect and desire God to show us what we need to know about ourselves, we will discover that he is slowly doing his work of conversion in our hearts, drawing us to himself.

In the group, share whatever experience you have of daily reflection.

Before doing this exercise in reflection on the day, re-read the six steps listed on pp.96–7 of this chapter.

Let someone read slowly **Jeremiah 29:11–13**.

Spend some time on your own, reflecting on the past day in this way. You may like to think of three positive occasions of feeling energised and connected. Then think of three negative occasions of feeling disintegrated or disconnected. You may wish, in silence, to confess your sin and ask God to forgive you.

In pairs, share as much of this as you want, or simply talk about what the reflection was like for you.

End the session by saying the Grace together.

DURING THE WEEK

Practise the Awareness Prayer each day and make notes of what you discover, what God shows you. Ask God to be in your reflection and to reveal himself to you, so that you can live more like Christ, whom you serve. Here is a simple outline for this kind of prayer.

Become still. Take time to become aware that you are in the presence of God, who loves you.

Thank the Lord for today and for the things about which you are particularly thankful.

Ask the Holy Spirit for grace to be aware of anything in the day which God wants to bring to your mind.

Do not struggle. Just let something surface as you allow your mind to recall the events of the day. Relive that experience, that meeting, those feelings. Ask Jesus what he wants you to see in it. Talk over with him what comes to mind and how you feel about what has been revealed. Be honest and allow the Lord time to speak to your heart.

Ask for grace for tomorrow to respond to God's love for you.

It can also be helpful periodically to reflect on the general pattern of your life over the past month or months. Try asking: What has God been doing in my life? How has he been leading me? What is he saying to me? How is he changing me?

Appendix 1: Notes for Group Leaders

Before the Group Meets Each Week

1. Pray regularly for the group members, and yourself, that God will bless the meetings and lead each person into a deeper relationship with him in prayer.
2. Pray for your preparation, that God will enable you to lead the group well.
3. Read the chapter in the book. Make a note of anything that you think will provoke questions or discussion.
4. Look through the study outline for the evening. Think about the timing remembering that the cassette will take about 12–14 minutes. Consider where you will have to keep carefully to your timing, or where you might want to adapt the outline for your particular group. Have a definite finishing time in mind. What could be omitted if time is short? Note that in session 3 choices will have to be made about which exercises to use. Some other study outlines have optional material.
5. Look carefully at the prayer exercises listed for the week following the group session. See if there is anything in the suggestions that is unclear. Try and work out what is meant in case group members need advice about how to tackle the exercises.
6. If you are going to use the cassette listen to the recorded interview for the particular week's theme and note anything that struck you or left you asking further questions. Have the cassette ready to play in the group meeting.
7. Think carefully about who will do refreshments and when they will be served.
8. Think carefully about the arrangement of chairs, bearing

in mind that people will be asked to share things in pairs and occasionally in threes. Seat everybody so that they can all see each other's faces. An ideal number for the group on a personal subject like prayer is between 6 and 10.

9. Try and ensure that each member of the group will have a copy of the book.

When the Group Meets

1. Arrive early so that you can welcome others as they arrive.
2. Get people to introduce themselves to each other.
3. At the first meeting agree with the group the regular finishing time.
4. Start the meeting with a simple prayer, asking for God to be present and to lead everyone into a deeper life of prayer.
5. Encourage everyone to participate fully, but reassure people that they may share only what they wish.
6. Don't talk too much yourself. Pauses for thought are good. Restrain others who talk too much, perhaps asking, 'Can we hear now from those who have not spoken (much)?'

When the Group is Over

1. Thank God for all that was good and encouraging in the meeting.
2. Think about any difficult moments and see if you have any ideas about what to do differently another time. If the group was difficult talk about it with someone who is experienced as a group leader. Where a church has several groups doing the course, it is best if there is a meeting from time to time with one of the ministers or an experienced lay leader, to share joys and problems.

Appendix 2: Leader's Guide for Imaginative Contemplation

Encourage everyone to try to visualise the scene and 'step into' the story as it unfolds, but not to worry if they can't. It is like getting into a radio play, or living in a film. Take a moment to settle, becoming relaxed and still.

(Read Luke 8:22–5 aloud to the group.)

Use the following, or other words, to guide people through the contemplation, remembering to leave long enough pauses (about 10–15 secs at each *, and 1–2 mins at each . . .). You should take 15–20 minutes over the whole contemplation.

Picture the scene: the hills, the lake and the boats. * Imagine yourself stepping into the scene. * Feel the breeze and sun on your skin. What can you see and hear? * You are there, with Jesus and the disciples. * You are near enough to hear Jesus say to the disciples, 'Let us go across to the other side of the lake.' You get into the boat with them. Where will you sit?. . .

As you sail along, Jesus lies down and goes to sleep. * The wind is beginning to get up. It feels cool. * Feel the boat rising and falling with the increasing waves. * Feel the cold, soaking spray as the waves crash onto the boat, which starts to fill with water. . . .

Sense the rising panic of the disciples, as the boat sinks lower into the water. * How are *you* feeling?. . .

And Jesus is still asleep. . . .

Someone wakes Jesus, saying, 'Master, we are perishing!' * How does Jesus seem, as he looks round at you all and takes in what is happening?. . .

How does Jesus deal with the situation? * How do you feel watching him rebuke the wind and the waves? * And as you experience the calm?. . .

Jesus is saying, 'Where is your faith?' How do you respond?. . .

The disciples say, 'Who is this, that even the wind and the waves obey him?' What are *you* wondering?. . .

As the boat proceeds, sit next to Jesus, if you can, and talk to him about what has happened and how you are feeling. . . .

You lapse into silence. Stay in the silence for as long as you want to, then gradually return to the group in the room.